The
WIDOW MAKER
Program

Extreme Self-Defense for Deadly Force Situations

Sammy Franco

The Widow Maker Program

Also by Sammy Franco

Maximum Damage: Hidden Secrets Behind Brutal Fighting Combinations
First Strike: End a Fight in Ten Seconds or Less!
Feral Fighting: Advanced Widow Maker Techniques
The Bigger They Are, The Harder They Fall
Self-Defense Tips and Tricks
Kubotan Power: Quick & Simple Steps to Mastering the Kubotan Keychain
The Complete Body Opponent Bag Book
Heavy Bag Training: Boxing, Mixed Martial Arts & Self-Defense
Gun Safety: For Home Defense and Concealed Carry
Out of the Cage: A Guide to Beating a Mixed Martial Artist on the Street
Warrior Wisdom: Inspiring Ideas from the World's Greatest Warriors
Judge, Jury and Executioner
Savage Street Fighting: Tactical Savagery as a Last Resort
War Craft: Street Fighting Tactics of the War Machine
War Machine: How to Transform Yourself Into a Vicious and Deadly Street Fighter
1001 Street Fighting Secrets
When Seconds Count: Self-Defense for the Real World
Killer Instinct: Unarmed Combat for Street Survival
Street Lethal: Unarmed Urban Combat

The Widow Maker Program: Extreme Self-Defense for Deadly Force Situations

Copyright © 2014 by Sammy Franco
ISBN: 978-1-941845-03-5
Printed in the United States of America

Published by Contemporary Fighting Arts, LLC.
P.O. Box 84028
Gaithersburg, Maryland 20883 USA
Phone: (301) 279-2244
Visit us Online at: www.SammyFranco.com

For author interviews or publicity information, please send inquiries in care of the publisher.

Contents

"He who does not punish evil commands it to be done."

- Leonardo Da Vinci

Warning!

The self-defense techniques, tactics, methods, and information described and depicted in this book can be dangerous and could result in serious injury and or death and should not be used or practiced in any way without the guidance of a professional reality based self-defense instructor.

The author, publisher, and distributors of this book disclaim any liability from loss, injury, or damage, personal or otherwise, resulting from the information and procedures in this book. *This book is for academic study only.*

Before you begin any exercise program, including those suggested in this book, it is important to check with your physician to see if you have any condition that might be aggravated by strenuous exercise.

Preface

The *Widow Maker Program* is a very unusual and unorthodox form of hand-to-hand combat. As a matter of fact, it's a revolutionary style of fighting that you won't find in any martial art school or self-defense class. The self-defense techniques featured in this fighting style are hard-core, indefensible, and utterly devastating. However, the true power of the Widow Maker Program comes from its ability to psychologically terrorize your adversary while simultaneously tearing him to pieces.

The objective of the Widow Maker Program is to teach you (the law-abiding citizen) how to use extreme force when faced with the immediate threat of unlawful deadly criminal attack. This combat program is also particularly useful for military personnel who require an efficient and effective way to eliminate a formidable enemy when engaged in unarmed combat.

The information presented in this book is ***not*** intended for sport combat, tournament competitions or any self-defense situation that does not justifiably warrant the use of deadly force.

Deadly force is defined as violent action known to create a substantial risk of causing death or serious bodily harm. A person may use deadly force in self-defense only if retaliating against another's deadly force.

Much of the information contained herein is lethal and should only be used to protect yourself or a loved one from immediate risk of unlawful deadly criminal attack. Remember, the decision to use deadly force must always be a last resort; after all other means of avoiding violence has been thoroughly exhausted.

The Widow Maker program consists of four chapters. Each one covers a critical aspect of my unique fighting methodology. In addition, since the lexicon in this book is defined within the context of the Widow Maker and its related elements, I have included a glossary of terms.

Like many of my previous publications, the Widow Maker program is both a skill-building workbook and strategic blueprint for combat. Feel free to write in the margins, underline passages, and dog-ear the pages.

Finally, I strongly recommend that you read this book from beginning to end, chapter by chapter. Only after you have read the entire book should you treat it like a reference and skip around, reading those sections or topics that interest you.

Welcome to the Widow Maker Program!

- Sammy Franco

Widow Maker Defined

WIDOW MAKER

Widow-maker \Wid"ow-mak`er\, n. One who makes widows by destroying husbands. [R.] --Shak.

Source: Webster's Revised Unabridged Dictionary, © 2014.

Chapter One
The Art of Webbing

The Widow Maker Program encompasses my two unique fighting methods: *Webbing* and *Razing*. Interestingly enough, both can serve as devastating "stand-alone" techniques that can effectively neutralize your attacker. However, when you combine these two methods of fighting into one seamless method of attack, you create an unstoppable force. Having said that, let's first look at webbing.

The Webbing Strike

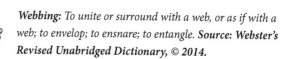

Webbing: To unite or surround with a web, or as if with a web; to envelop; to ensnare; to entangle. **Source: Webster's Revised Unabridged Dictionary, © 2014.**

The Widow Maker Program

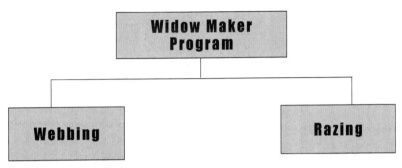

The Widow Maker Program is comprised of two fighting methods: webbing and razing.

The webbing technique is unique to my Contemporary Fighting Arts (CFA) self-defense system. To some, it might look like nothing more than a reinforced palm heel strike. But in reality, it's much more than that!

As you will learn, the body mechanics and footwork required to deliver a proper webbing strike differ drastically from the standard or "run of the mill" palm heel. In actuality, comparing the palm heel strike to the webbing technique is like comparing a 9mm handgun to a Howitzer.

I have named this technique "webbing" because your hands resemble a large web that wraps around the opponent's face. Webbing is also a multi-purpose combat technique that serves several functions in unarmed combat. Some include the following:

- **Entry Tool** - In order to apply the razing method of fighting, you first need to get close to your adversary. Unfortunately, numerous fights will begin outside of close-quarters combat range (CQC). You must find a way to safely close the distance gap between you and your adversary. Fortunately, webbing can be used as a *safe and dependable entry tool* to CQC range (the distance where razing techniques are applied).

- **First Strike Weapon** - Like I stated earlier, webbing is a devastating "stand-alone" striking technique. It's virtually undetectable when executed, making it an ideal candidate for a first strike weapon. When delivered correctly, the webbing strike is safe, efficient and extremely effective striking technique. As a matter of fact, if the webbing technique is delivered correctly, your adversary will become instantaneously disabled.

- **Sets Up Razing** - If your webbing strike doesn't knock-out your adversary, it will most certainly soften him up (physically and psychologically) for the second phase of attack - razing!

- **Defensive Tool** - Webbing can actually be used as a defensive response against an attack and it's particularly effective when used in conjunction with my de-escalation stance.

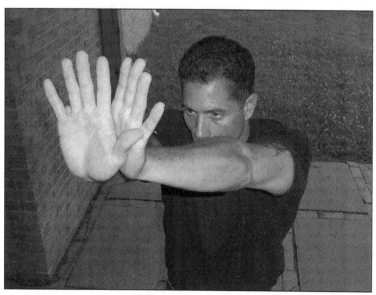

The webbing technique is the heavy artillery of hand strikes. Here, Sammy Franco demonstrates the proper hand and arm positioning for the technique. Also observe that his head is slightly angled down.

3

WEBBING APPLICATIONS

- **Entry tool to CQC range**
- **First strike weapon**
- **Sets up Razing**
- **Defensive Tool**

Here, the author demonstrates how the webbing strike can be used as both an entry tool and defensive technique at the same time. Notice the protection offered to both his face and head.

If your adversary attacks while you are delivering the webbing strike, his blows will be deflected over or around your head. This leaves your eyes, nose, chin, temple and throat protected from attack.

4

The Webbing Stance

Theoretically you can launch the webbing strike from any standing posture, however there are two ideal stances that will maximize your odds of successfully landing a devastating hit. They are: First Strike and Natural stance.

As I have mentioned in my previous books, a skilled fighter will never stand squarely in front of his adversary. If the opportunity is presented, you should always try to assume a strategic stance. Remember, a stance defines your ability to defend or attack your enemy and it can play a substantive role in the outcome of a street

STANCE ADVANTAGES

- **It minimizes target exposure**
- **It enhances your balance when fighting**
- **It promotes rapid foot work and mobility**
- **It amplifies striking power**
- **Provides kinesthetic and psychological reference point for proper webbing deployment**
- **Court defensible physiology**
- **Reduces possibility of witness intervention**

Webbing is considered a deadly force self-defense technique and should be used in life and death situations that warrant the use of deadly force. Remember, always be certain your actions are legally and morally justified in the eyes of the law!

fight.

A strategic stance is crucial for effective webbing for some of the following reasons:

- It minimizes your target exposure
- It enhances your balance when fighting
- It promotes rapid foot work and mobility
- It amplifies striking power
- It provides both a kinesthetic and psychological reference point for webbing deployment

Just remember, a stance in a true luxury in combat. There will be situations and circumstances that will not afford you the opportunity of assuming a stance. So always be prepared to deploy your webbing strike without any foundational structure. Having said that, lets take a look at some of the strategic postures you can use with the webbing technique.

Believe it or not, the webbing strike can also be used when ground fighting with the adversary.

The First Strike Stance

The webbing stance is used prior to initiating your strike. It facilitates "invisible deployment" of a webbing strike while simultaneously protecting your vital targets against various possible counter attacks. This stance is almost identical to my de-escalation and first strike stances. The proper webbing stance is acquired first angling your body at approximately 45-degrees from the enemy. Then keep both of your feet roughly shoulder-width apart and have your knees slightly bent with your weight evenly distributed.

Your hand positioning is another critical component of the webbing stance. When faced with an opponent in the kicking and punching ranges of unarmed combat, keep both of your hands open, relaxed and up to protect the upper gates of your centerline. Both of your palms should be facing the opponent with both arms bent approximately 100 degrees. This arm positioning is critical because it "loads" the webbing strike. When faced with an adversary in grappling range, keep both of your hands a bit

Pictured here, the first strike stance.

closer to your body and maintain the same leg positioning.

Also remember to keep your torso, pelvis, head, and back erect and stay relaxed and alert—while remaining at ease and in total control of your emotions and body. Be sure to avoid any muscular tension—don't tighten up your shoulders, neck, arms, or thighs (tension restricts breathing and quick evasive movement, and it will quickly sap your vital energy).

The Natural Stance

The webbing strike can also be launched from the Natural Stance. The Natural stance is often used when approached by an individual (i.e., drunken bum, street vagrant, typical stranger, etc.) who appears non-threatening, yet very suspicious.

To assume this stance, angle your body 45-degrees from the suspicious individual and keep both of your feet approximately shoulder-width apart. Your knees should be slightly bent with your weight evenly distributed. Keep both of your hands in front of your body with some type of natural movement (e.g.,

Here, the author demonstrates the natural stance.

8

rub your hands together, scratch your wrist, or scratch your temple), which will help protect your upper targets from a possible attack. Do remember to stay relaxed but alert, avoiding any muscular tension in your shoulders, neck, or arms. Under no circumstances should you ever drop your hands below your chest level when assuming a natural stance. While this may seem like a "natural posture" it offers too many vulnerabilities that can be exploited by your adversary.

The Webbing Target

The webbing strike is delivered specifically to the enemy's chin. This anatomical target is ideal because when struck at a forty-five degree angle, shock waves are transmitted to the cerebellum and cerebral hemispheres of the brain, resulting in paralysis and immediate unconsciousness. Other possible injuries include broken jaw, concussion, whiplash to the neck, broken neck, permanent paralysis, coma and death.

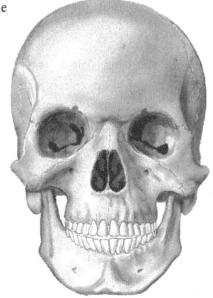

Webbing should never be delivered to the opponent's collarbone, chest or stomach. Such anatomical targets will yield poor results and simply enrage your adversary.

The target for the webbing strike is the opponent's mandible (chin).

The Widow Maker Program

Striking the opponent's chin at a 45 degree angle will maximize damage to his brain and cervical vertebra.

Important! The only viable target for the webbing strike is the opponent's chin.

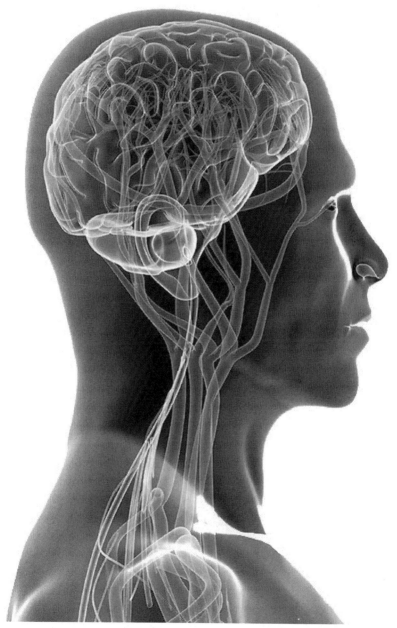

While the chin is your exterior target, the ultimate objective is to send shock waves to the opponent's brain.

Webbing Body Mechanics

The webbing strike is not just a matter of simply launching a double palm heel strike at the enemy. There is a lot more to it than that. It does require precise hand and arm articulation, proper body mechanics and correct timing. However, once mastered, webbing will feel natural and will become an instinctual body weapon that can be delivered under the stress of a deadly criminal attack.

What follows is a detailed breakdown of the proper body mechanics for effective webbing. Keep in mind, proper webbing body mechanics should take less than one second to execute.

Step 1. From a right lead (your right leg is forward) stance. Simultaneously overlap your left hand on top of your right hand. Your right thumb should be lined under the 5th metacarpal of your left hand (see illustration). Your right palm is the striking surface while your left reinforces the structural integrity of the strike. The left hand is also particularly important because it significantly reduces the risk of a wrist or hand injury and it magnifies the power of the blow.

To avoid finger jams and breaks when delivering the webbing strike, make certain to have your palms perpendicular to the ground.

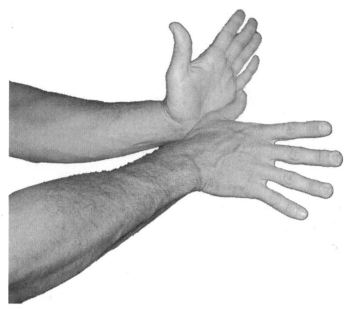

When performing a right hand webbing strike, be certain your right thumb is placed under the 5th metacarpal of your left hand.

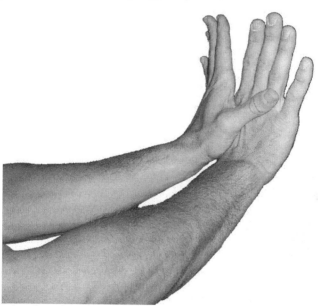

In this photo, the right palm is the striking surface while your left reinforces the structural integrity of the strike.

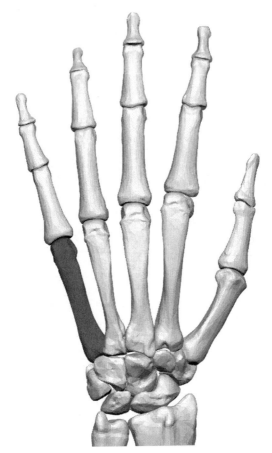

Illustration: Bones of the left hand. Dorsal surface. The 5th metacarpal is shaded.

Step 2. Once the hands are correctly joined, forcefully extend both arms into the enemy's chin. Your elbows should also be slightly bent when impacting with the target. Do not completely lock your elbows. Unlike conventional punches, your body does not torque when launching the webbing strike. Destructive power comes from the synergistic use of your major muscle groups (i.e., back, chest, shoulders and triceps) accompanied with forward momentum.

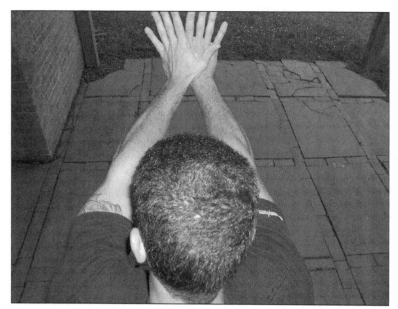

When the webbing strike is executed properly, your arms and shoulders should resemble an isosceles triangle.

Step 3. The trajectory of the webbing blow should be approximately 45-degrees to the enemy's chin. Remember, you are trying to transmit shock waves to the cerebellum and cerebral hemispheres of the assailant's brain. Make sure that both of your palms are perpendicular to the floor. This palm alignment will minimize finger sprains and ensure flush contact with the target.

Do not torque or twist your body when delivering the webbing strike. This will compromise the structural integrity of your hand positioning and the accuracy of your strike.

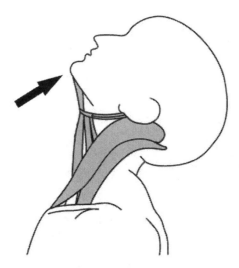

The webbing strike should be delivered at a 45-degree angle to the opponent's chin.

Step 4. You can launch the webbing strike while remaining stationary, however forward momentum will increase the power exponentially. Forward momentum can be generated in one of two ways: the Half Step and Full Step.

The Half Step - this movement generates significant striking power. To perform the half step, your lead foot moves forward approximately 24 inches, while the rear foot remains stationary.

The Full Step – this movement generates maximum striking power. To perform the full step, move your front foot forward (approximately 24 inches) and then move your rear foot an equal distance.

Practice both the full and half step footwork daily for 10 to 15 minutes in front of a full-length mirror until your footwork is explosive, balanced and natural.

Webbing Footwork: The Half Step

Pictured here, the starting position for the half step.

To perform the half step, move your lead foot forward approximately 24 inches, while the rear foot remain stationary.

The Full Step

Pictured here, the starting position for the full step.

To perform the full step, move your lead foot forward approximately 24 inches, let your rear foot follow an equal distance.

It's very important to properly time your footwork with the webbing strike. Remember, both of your arms must join together simultaneously as you step forward.

Step 5. Once the two hands make solid contact with the target, allow both hands to split apart. Your left hand grasps the nape of the opponent's neck (this is referred to as "anchoring") while the right hand begins to raze the adversary. See Chapter 2 for more information about Anchoring.

Webbing Demonstration

Step 1: Begin from a first strike stance.

Step 2: Simultaneously overlap your left hand on top of your right hand. Your right thumb should be lined under the 5th metacarpal of your left hand.

Step 3: Once your hands are properly joined, forcefully extend both of your arms forward.

Step 4: Drop your head slightly downward as you step forward.

Step 5: Make certain your elbows are slightly bent when impacting with the target.

Full Contact Webbing Demonstration

Step 1: The defender (left) assumes a first strike stance.

Step 2: In one fluid motion, he joins both hands together, extends both arms and moves forward.

Step 3: The webbing strike makes contact with the opponent's target.

Webbing Technique Review

Step 1. From a right lead (your right leg is forward) stance. Simultaneously overlap your left hand on top of your right hand. Your right thumb should be lined under the 5th metacarpal of your left hand (see illustration). Your right palm is the striking surface while your left reinforces the structural integrity of the strike. The left hand is also particularly important because it significantly reduces the likelihood of a wrist or hand injury and it magnifies the power of the blow.

Step 2. Once the hands are properly joined, forcefully extend both arms into the enemy's chin. Your elbows should also be slightly bent when impacting with the target. Do not completely lock your elbows. Unlike conventional punches, your body does not torque when launching the webbing strike. Destructive power comes from the synergistic use of your major muscle groups (i.e., back, chest, shoulders and triceps) accompanied with forward momentum.

Step 3. The trajectory of the webbing blow should be approximately 45-degrees to the enemy's chin. Remember, you are trying to transmit shock waves to the cerebellum and cerebral hemispheres of the assailant's brain. Make certain that both of your palms are perpendicular to the floor. This palm alignment will minimize finger sprains and maximize flush contact with the target.

Step 4. You can launch the webbing strike while remaining stationary, however forward momentum will increase the power exponentially. Forward momentum can be generated in one of two ways: the Half Step and Full Step.

Step 5. Once the two hands make solid contact with the target, allow both hands to split apart. Your left hand grasps the nape of the opponent's neck (this is referred to as "anchoring") while the right hand begins to raze the adversary.

If you intend on transitioning into the razing method of attack, do not retract the webbing strike. Retracting the webbing strike negates the economy of motion, breaks the offensive flow and diminishes the feral characteristics of your attack. Unlike conventional punches and strikes, the webbing strike should split apart, allowing you to anchor the opponent and flow into razing.

Don't Confuse Webbing with the "V" Grip

It's common for some people to confuse the webbing strike with the "V" grip. While the two may look similar, they are very different from each other. The "V" grip is used when you are unarmed and defending against an edged weapon attack. It requires that you place your thumb under the first metacarpal (not the fifth) when applying the technique (see photo below).

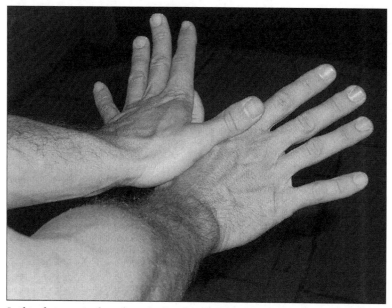

In this photo, notice how the right thumb is aligned under the 1st metacarpal of the left hand (not the 5th) when configuring the "V" grip.

Defending against a knife attack is extremely dangerous. However, you can learn more about the "V" grip and its application during unarmed knife encounters by visiting my website at: SammyFranco.com.

The Widow Maker Program

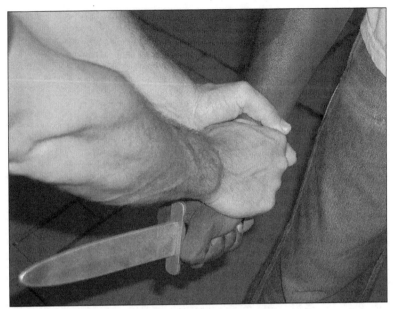

The "V" grip is the foundation of unarmed knife defense, don't confuse it with the Widow Maker Program.

Chapter Two
Bridging the Gap

Anchoring the Opponent

After hitting the opponent with the webbing technique, you must **anchor** him. Essentially, anchoring means controlling and preventing the opponent from disengaging the range of engagement. Remember, for the Widow Maker program to work effectively, you must maintain close-quarter combat range and keep the pressure on the adversary.

Anchoring is also essential because it effectively bridges the gap between the webbing and razing methodologies. There are two variations of anchoring that you need to be familiar with: Offense and Defense. Let's look at each one.

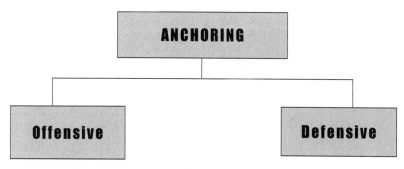

There are two variations of anchoring: offensive and defensive.

Offensive Anchoring

Offenses anchoring is carried out immediately after you have delivered the webbing strike. It requires you to grab hold of your opponent's neck with one hand while performing the razing technique with your other free hand. Anchoring is critical for effective razing skills for the following five reasons:

1. It maintains the range for effective and continuous razing.

2. It prevents the opponent from disengaging CQC range.

3. It stabilizes the assailant's head allowing maximum pressure against both eye and throat targets when executing zero beat techniques.

4. It provides a "tactile" reference point if your vision is impaired during the course of the fight.

5. It establishes and transmits "Alpha" or "Predator" body language to the enemy.

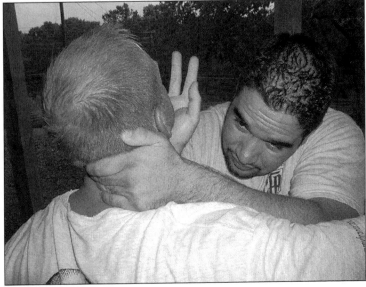

Here, a student demonstrates offensive anchoring. Anchoring bridges the gap between webbing and razing.

Offensive Anchoring Demonstration

Step 1: The author assumes a first strike stance.

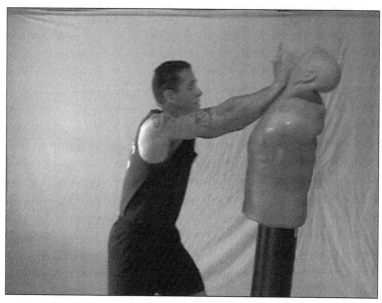

Step 2: He executes a webbing strike to the body opponent bag.

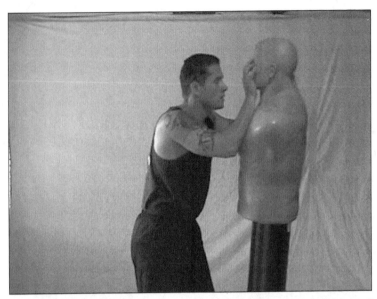

Step 3: Once contact is made with the target, Franco's left hand grasps the nape of the neck while his right hand begins the razing technique.

Transitioning from Webbing to Anchoring

The following photos demonstrate the proper way to transition from webbing to anchoring.

Step 1: Once your webbing strike makes contact with the opponent's chin, split your hands apart and move your left hand to the back of the opponent's neck.

Step 2: Firmly grasp the back of the opponent neck (anchoring) with your left hand.

Step 3: Once your offensive anchor is secure, begin razing the opponent's face.

Besides preventing your opponent from disengaging CQC range, offensive anchoring also amplifies the damage of your razing skills by forcing the opponent's face into your attacking limbs.

Switching Anchor Positions

There will be situations when you will need to switch anchors during the course of your razing assault. For example, you might injure your razing hand and need to switch hands in order to maintain the offensive flow. Or, your adversary might force you to change anchoring positions. The following photo sequence demonstrates the proper way to switch neck anchors.

Anchor Switching Demonstration

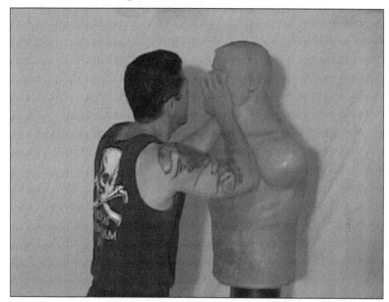

Step 1: Begin with a left hand anchor position.

Step 2: Remove your left anchoring position and simultaneously raze the opponent with both of your hands. Remember to maintain significant forward pressure.

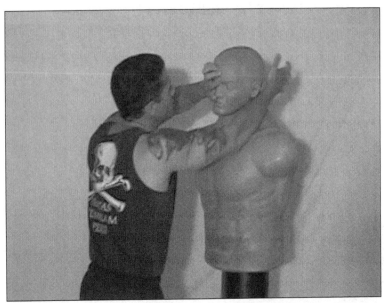

Step 3: While razing, move your right hand behind the opponent's neck.

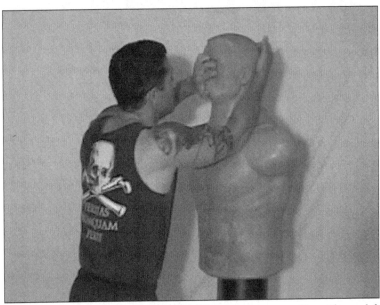

Step 4: Firmly secure the opponent's neck while continuing to raze him with your left hand.

Defensive Anchoring

Next, is defensive anchoring which is used in remote cases when you're razing assault is broken and the opponent retaliates with a barrage of strikes.

Defensive anchoring requires you to grab hold of the opponent's neck with both of your hands while dropping your head between both of your biceps. Defensive anchoring is a temporary protective posture that hides your head and nullifying the opponent's strikes.

Best of all, it still enables you to control the opponent and prevent him from disengaging the range. The objective is to protect your head from attack until you can control one of the opponent's arms.

Here, Sammy Franco demonstrates the hand positioning required for defensive anchoring.

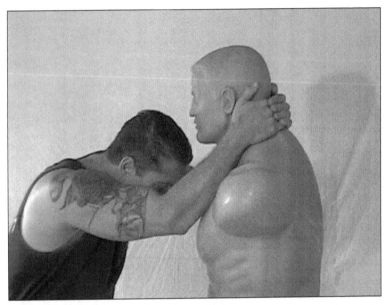

Here, the author demonstrates defensive anchoring. Notice how his head is angled down.

Defensive anchoring is a quick defensive measure that should only be performed for a brief second, until you can gain control of one of the opponent's arms.

Anchor Points

As I stated earlier, the ideal anchoring point is the opponent's neck. The neck offers the greatest amount of stability and control over the opponent. However, under some circumstances, you can also anchor the opponent's upper arm. Under no circumstances should you ever anchor the opponent's clothing. Clothing can easily be torn and provides absolutely no control over the opponent.

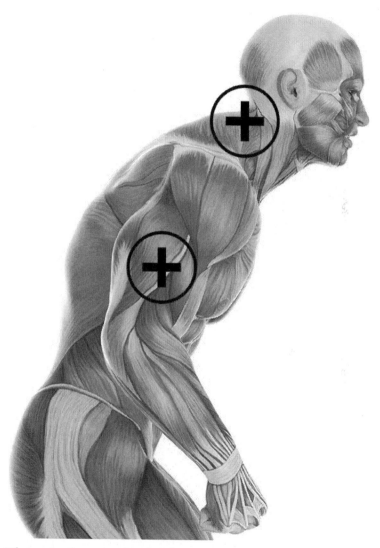

When razing, the opponent's neck and upper arms are your primary anchor points.

Anchoring the Upper Arm

Anchoring the opponent's upper arm often occurs from a defensive anchor position. For example, say you have successfully launched the webbing strike, moved into CQC range and secured the opponent's neck. However, before you commence with razing, your offensive flow is broken and the opponent retaliates with a barrage of strikes. In such a situation, you must prioritize defense by dropping your head down and establishing a defensive anchor position.

Once you are in a defensive anchor position, you'll need to intercept one of your opponent's blows and trap it under your arm using a windmill trapping motion. Once this is accomplished you will have successfully anchored the upper arm and now have the freedom to counterattack with razing.

To give you a better idea how this is accomplished, see the arm anchoring demonstration.

Arm Anchoring Demonstration

In this scenario, the defender (left) controls his opponent with a defensive anchor.

The opponent (right) continues to swing wildly.

The defender is safe and protected as his opponent continues to swing at him.

At the proper moment, the defender wraps his left arm (windmill motion) around his opponent's right arm.

Once the defender secures and traps his opponent's right arm, he uses it as an anchor point and begins razing.

The defender continues to raze his opponent until it is safe to secure the neck anchor.

While the opponent's neck is the best target for anchoring, you can also anchor the opponent's upper arm. Do not anchor the opponent's clothing.

Wrist Anchoring

Sometimes the opponent will unknowingly set up an anchor point for you. For example, a common reaction dynamic when being raised is for the opponent to grab hold of your attacking hand and pull it away from his face. In essence, your adversary is unintentionally creating another anchoring point (your wrist). In such a circumstance, you will be required to switch anchors to resume your razing assault.

Wrist Anchoring Demonstration

Step 1: Sammy Franco razes his opponent with his right hand.

Step 2: The opponent grabs Franco's wrist and pulls his hand down.

Step 3: Franco presses his right arm firmly against the opponent's body and begins razing with his left hand.

Step 4: Franco continues to raze his opponent until he releases his wrist.

Step 5: When the opponent releases his grab, Franco anchors the neck and resumes razing with his right hand.

There are some circumstances where you won't need to anchor your adversary. For example, if he is backed against a wall or your are mounted on top of him during a ground fight.

The Widow Maker Program

Chapter Three
The Science of Razing

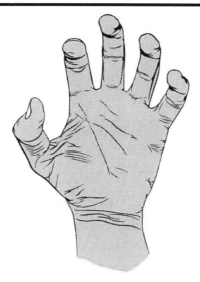

Razing

Once you have landed the webbing strike and have successfully anchored your opponent, you must immediately flow into the razing method of attack. Again, it's critical that you don't permit your offensive flow to break for even a second. The fundamental objective is to harmoniously amalgamate webbing and razing into one relentless and strategically calculated assault. In turn, this will short circuit the opponent's cognitive brain function. Essentially, he's screwed!

Raze: 1. *To erase; to efface; to obliterate.* 2. *To subvert from the foundation; to lay level with the ground; to destroy; to demolish. Source: Webster's Revised Unabridged Dictionary,* © 2014.

When transitioning from webbing to razing, it's critical to maintain the offensive flow and keep the pressure on the opponent. Don't let your assault break for even a second.

We're Not in Kansas Anymore!

I've been teaching reality based self-defense (RBSD) for over thirty years and I can say, with one-hundred percent confidence, that razing is the most devastating form of unarmed fighting know to man. Its brutal and invasive characteristics are both physically and psychologically traumatic for the recipient. The overwhelming nature of razing invokes instantaneous panic by delivering a destructiveness exceeding that of a deadly and evil criminal aggressor.

When razing is properly performed, it accomplishes the following objectives:

1. **Cognitive Brain Shutdown** - The brutal and overwhelming nature of razing overrides the opponent's cognitive brain preventing him from any lucid thought process. Since razing is so fast and ferocious, the opponent's cognitive brain can't process what is happening to him.

2. **Instant Damage** - Razing is simply indefensible! The speed and proximity at which these quarter beat hits are delivered is truly overwhelming. The bottom line is, they are just too fast and too close for the opponent to react defensively. In many ways, razing is likened to an angry swarm of wasps, your only hope is to try and escape from the pain.

More Advantages of Razing

There are many other advantages to adding my razing methodology to your current self-defense training. What follows is a brief list:

1. ***It's unconventional*** - *razing is a very unusual and unorthodox form of fighting. Even the most seasoned martial artist or street fighter has never been exposed to this unconventional style of combat. As a result, they are unprepared to handle it both physically and psychologically.*

2. ***Low maintenance*** - *razing techniques are exceptionally efficient and easy to perform under the duress of real world combat conditions. Unlike kicking and punching, you don't need to spend countless hours perfecting fine motor skill body mechanics.*

3. ***Less chance of injuries*** - *unlike fisted blows, you don't run the risk of spraining or breaking your wrists or hands when performing razing techniques.*

Exactly What is Razing?

In Contemporary Fighting Arts, *razing* is defined as a series of vicious close quarter techniques designed to physically and psychologically extirpate a criminal attacker. These close quarter techniques are executed at various beats: (half beat, quarter beat and zero beat) and they include the following:

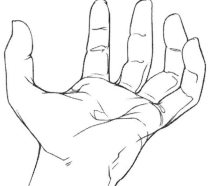

- Eye raking

- Eye gouging

- Tearing

- Crushing
- Biting
- Hair pulling
- Elbow strikes
- Shaving forearms
- Head butts
- Hair Pulling
- Bicep pops
- Neck cranks
- Finishing chokes

To the uninitiated, razing will appear bizarre, haphazard, and chaotic. Some might erroneously assume it's a "gross motor skill" method of fighting. However, nothing can be farther from the truth. Razing is a close-quarter fighting method that requires technical precision, timing, and strategic implementation. Razing is also a culmination of several advanced "techniques" that do require training and practice to master.

However, this is not to say that you can't just "wing it" and barrage the opponent with a series of gross motor razing technique. It can be done and, in some cases, improvising razing will yield results. However, to really unleash the sheer devastating power of razing, you

One of the greatest advantages of razing is that it's a very unusual form of fighting that people have never seen before. As a result, they are unprepared to handle it both physically and psychologically.

must learn to deliver it in a tactical and calculated manner.

Best of all, razing is straightforward and can easily be integrated into any style of fighting. If you currently study Krav Maga, Jeet Kune Do, Mixed Martial Arts, Karate or Kung-Fu, you can seamlessly merge razing into your style or system.

When Can I Raze?

I would be remiss if I did not give you a few caveats about razing. First, because of its devastating power, razing should only be used in self-defense situations that warrant the application of deadly force.

Understanding Deadly Force

So what is deadly force? First, let me state that you must never use force against anyone unless it is absolutely necessary. Next, *"force"* is broken down into two levels: deadly and non deadly. Deadly force is defined as violent action known to create a substantial risk of causing death or serious bodily harm. A person may use deadly force in self-defense only if retaliating against another's deadly force. Non deadly force is an amount of force that does not result in serious bodily injury or death.

Let me be clear, both webbing and razing can produce serious bodily harm and possible death. They are classified as deadly force techniques and must only be used to protect yourself or a loved one from immediate risk of unlawful deadly criminal attack. Remember,

The physical residuals from razing are horrid. In many cases, you will permanently disfigure your opponent's facial anatomy. Therefore, you must be absolutely certain that your self-defense actions are legally and morally justified in the eyes of the law!

the decision to use deadly force must always be a last resort; after all other means of avoiding violence has been thoroughly exhausted.

Razing should not be used as an intermediate use-of-force tactic. It is not designed to be "toned down" as a compliance tool to gain control over your opponent. It's all or nothing with razing! For it to work effectively, it must be delivered with tremendous force and blistering speed. Frankly, anything less will likely result in the opponent seriously injuring you.

Understanding Widow Maker's Beat System

In order to truly appreciate the razing method of attack, you need to have a fundamental understanding of my beat system. Essentially, there are four (4) beat classifications. They include:

- **Full Beat** - your strike has an initiation and retraction phase. (Standard punches and blows are generally considered "full beat strikes." For example, lead straight, rear cross, etc.)

- **Half Beat** - your strike is delivered through the retraction phase of the proceeding strike.

- **Quarter Beat** - a rapid series of strikes that never break contact with the target. Quarter beat strikes are primary

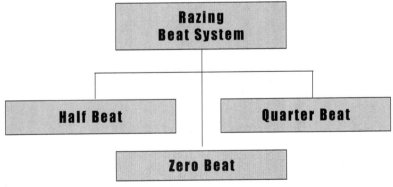

Razing techniques are executed at three different beats.

responsible for creating the psychological panic and trauma for the opponent.

- **Zero Beat** - full pressure techniques applied to a specific target until it completely ruptures. Includes gouging, biting and choking techniques. Primary anatomical targets include: the eyes and throat. Zero beat is most often applied at the end of your razing assault.

While there are four unique beat classifications, the razing methodology only uses three. They are: half, quarter and full beats.

Don't confuse the Widow Maker's beat system with the one discussed in Bruce Lee's Tao of Jeet Kune Do. Pictured here, a statute of the great Bruce Lee.

While all three beat classifications are important to the Widow Maker program, it's the quarter beat that evokes panic in your adversary.

Full Beat Demonstration

Step 1: Franco squares off in a fighting stance.

Step 2: He delivers a lead straight punch by extending his arm at his opponent.

Step 3: Franco retracts his arm back to the starting position.

Half Beat Demonstration

Step 1: Franco assumes a fighting stance.

Step 2: He delivers a lead palm heel strike by extending his arm.

Step 3: As Franco retracts his arm back, he converts it to a lead horizontal elbow strike.

Quarter Beat Demonstration

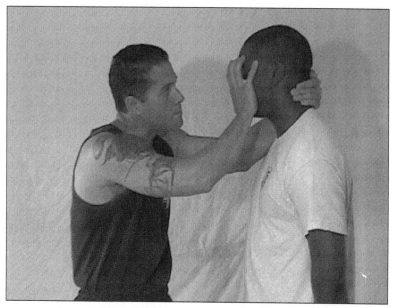

Step 1: Franco begins his quarter beat assault with an eye rake.

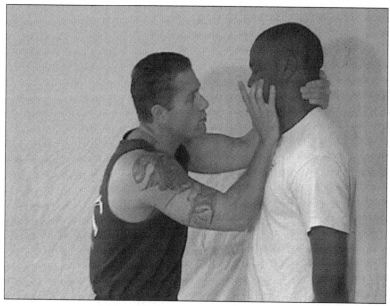

Step 2: He rakes the opponent's eyes in a quick downward motion.

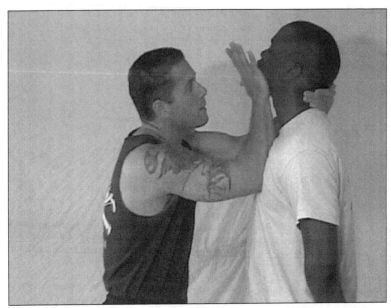

Step 3: Without breaking contact with his opponent's face, he attacks with a palm jolt to the chin.

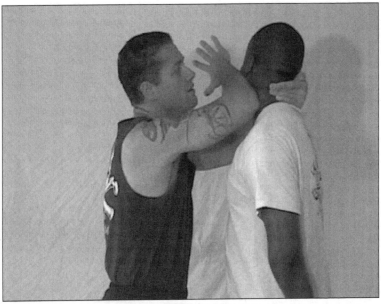

Step 4: He immediately follows up with a shaving forearm across his opponent's face.

Zero Beat Demonstration

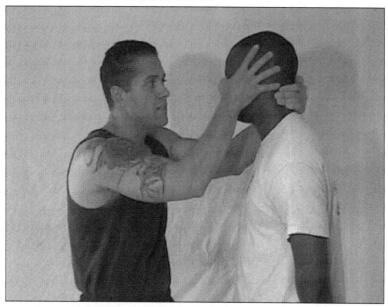

Pictured here, the author demonstrates a single thumb gouge technique.

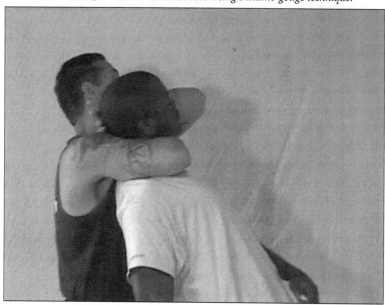

The rear naked choke (RNC) is another effective zero beat technique used at the completion phase of razing.

The Widow Maker Program

The zero beat should always be used at the end of your razing sequence. This can be in the form of a choke, eye rupture or throat crush.

Razing Techniques

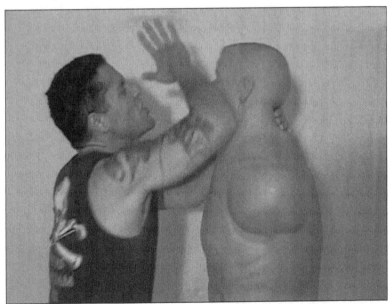

The Shaving Forearm.

The Eye Rake.

The Short Arc Hammer Fist.

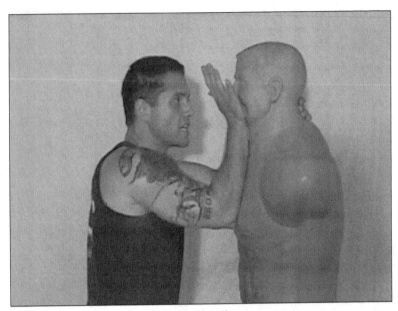

The Palm Jolt.

The Thumb Gouge.

The Vertical Elbow.

The Horizontal Elbow.

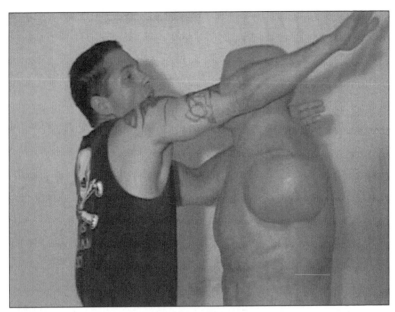

The Biceps Pop.

Biting.

The Head Butt.

The Throat Crush.

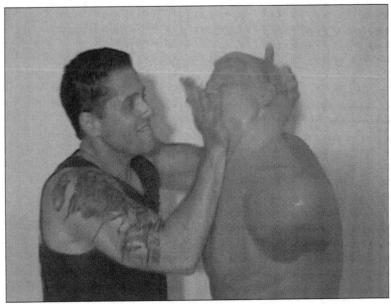

The Neck Crank.

What about Kicking Techniques?

Do not attempt kicking techniques when razing your adversary. As a matter of fact, if you attempt to kick during your razing sequence, you'll break the offensive flow and put yourself in serious jeopardy.

As I stated earlier, the real power of razing comes from your ability to shock the opponent and force his cognitive brain to temporarily "shutdown." In order to accomplish this, you must always keep the pressure on the opponent. Unfortunately, kicking techniques take you out of close-quarter combat range and offers the adversary an opportunity to immediately retaliate.

While kicking can be useful in a fight, it should not be used when razing your adversary.

What about Knee Strikes?

Avoid the urge to knee strike your adversary when performing razing techniques. Knee strikes are simply too risky to employ.

You must remember that razing techniques will almost always force your opponent to frantically pull away from your attack. Delivering a knee strike, while the opponent pulls away, will compromise the integrity of your stance and cause you to lose your balance.

More importantly, delivering a knee strike during a razing sequence will momentarily break your offensive flow. The bottom line is, avoid knee strikes when razing your adversary!

Chest to Back Position

The chest to back position is the ideal place to be when you complete your razing assault. It offers maximum control of your opponent while minimizing his ability to effectively counter strike. More importantly, the chest to back position enables you to apply a devastating rear naked choke (RNC) technique.

However, this is not to say that you must always have a chest to back position to end the fight. It's just a strategically preferred location.

You can acquire the chest to back position in one of two ways: a reflexive turn or by applying the neck crank technique.

- **Reflexive Turn** - When you raze the adversary his cognitive brain will shutdown and he will reflexively turn away from the attack. The opponent is exclusively focused on avoiding the pain of your quarter beat strikes, he often does not realize that he's making a huge strategic error by exposing his back during the fight.

- **Neck Crank Technique** - You can also acquire the chest to back position by applying the neck crank technique at the end of your razing sequence. I have a saying, "When the neck turns, the body follows."

While the chest to back position is the ideal place to end your razing assault, it's not a mandatory position.

Neck Crank Demonstration

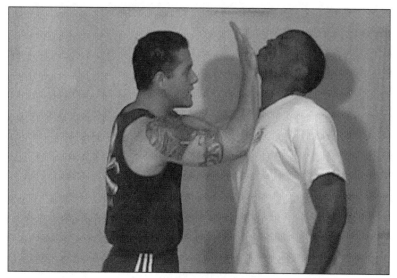

Step 1: Begin with your palm pressed against the opponent's chin.

Step 2: Next, push your opponent's chin in a counter clockwise direction.

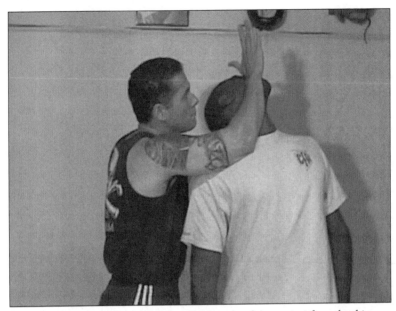

Step 3: As your opponent's head and body turn, release contact from the chin.

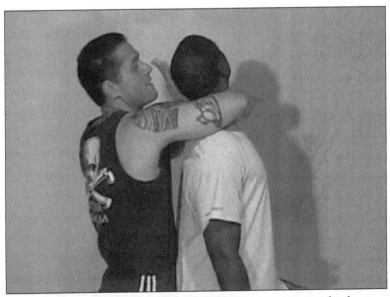

Step 4: Once the opponent exposes his back, insert your arm against this throat.

Step 5: Solidify the rear naked choke hold.

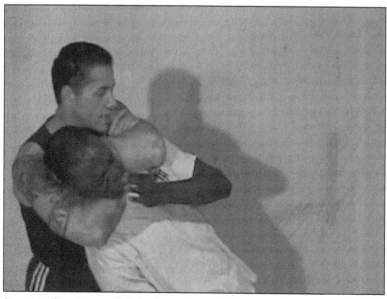

Step 6: Apply pressure with both of your arms while forcing the opponent to the ground.

Razing Targets

Razing techniques require you to attack a very specific set of anatomical targets. All of these targets can be found on the opponent's face and head. They include the following:

- **Eyes**
- **Temple**
- **Nose**
- **Chin**
- **Throat**
- **Neck**

Let's begin by looking at each target. We will start with the opponent's eyes.

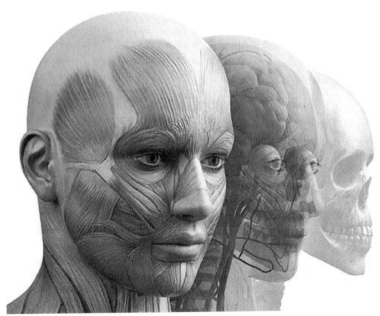

All of your razing targets can be found on the opponent's face and head.

EYES

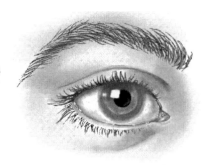

Eyes sit in the orbital bones of the skull. They are ideal targets for razing because they are extremely sensitive and difficult to protect, and damaging them requires very little force. The eyes can be poked, scratched, and gouged from a variety of angles. Depending on the force of your strike, it can cause numerous injuries, including:

- watering of the eyes
- hemorrhaging,
- blurred vision
- temporary or permanent blindness
- severe pain
- rupture
- shock
- unconsciousness

TEMPLE

The temple or sphenoid bone is a thin, weak bone located on the side of the skull approximately 1 inch from the eyes. Because of its fragile structure and close proximity to the brain, a powerful strike to this target can be deadly. Other injuries include

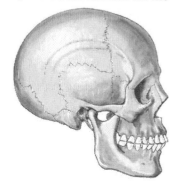

- unconsciousness
- hemorrhage

- concussion
- shock
- coma

NOSE

The nose is made up of a thin bone, cartilage, numerous blood vessels, and many nerves. It's a particularly good target for razing because it stands out from the opponent's face and can be struck from three different directions (up, straight, down). A powerful blow can cause:

- stunning pain
- eye-watering
- temporary blindness
- hemorrhaging
- shock
- unconsciousness

CHIN

The chin is equally a good target for razing techniques. When it is struck at a 45-degree angle, shock is transmitted to the cerebellum and cerebral hemispheres of the brain, resulting in paralysis and immediate unconsciousness. Other possible injuries include:

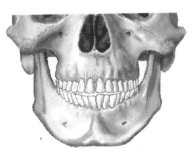

- broken jaw

- concussion

- whiplash to the neck

THROAT

The throat is a lethal razing
target because it is only protected
by a thin layer of skin. This region
consists of the thyroid, hyaline
and crocoid cartilage, trachea, and
larynx. The trachea, or windpipe, is a
cartilaginous tube that measures 4 1/2
inches in length and is approximately
1 inch in diameter. A powerful strike
to this target can result in:

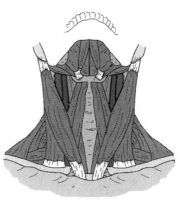

- unconsciousness

- blood drowning

- massive hemorrhaging

- air starvation

- death

If the thyroid cartilage is crushed, hemorrhaging will occur, the
windpipe will quickly swell shut, resulting in suffocation.

*Important: The mouth is not a viable razing target. Do not
attempt any type of fish-hooking techniques when razing
your adversary. Keep you fingers out of the opponent's
mouth or you can lose a digit.*

BACK OF NECK

The back of the neck consists of the first seven vertebrae of the spinal column. They act as a circuit board for nerve impulses from the brain to the body. The back of the neck is a lethal target because the vertebrae are poorly protected. A quick and forceful twisting of the neck can cause:

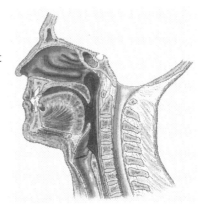

- shock
- unconsciousness
- a broken neck
- complete paralysis
- coma
- death

The opponent's neck serves as both an anchoring point as well as a zero beat target.

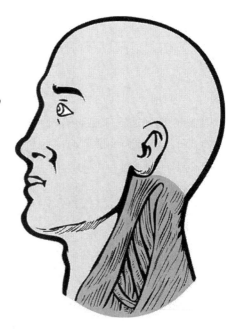

Probable Reaction Dynamics from Razing

In my book, *Maximum Damage: Hidden Secrets Behind Brutal Fighting Combinations,* I discussed the critical importance of mastering "probable reaction dynamics." Basically, probable reaction dynamics refer to your opponent's anticipated or predicted movements or actions during combat.

Probable reaction dynamics awareness is also a vital component of razing. As a matter of fact, your entire razing sequence is predicated on how your opponent reacts to your hits. Each of one of the opponent's physical reactions will determine each one of your quarter beat strikes. Remember, *razing techniques are not memorized or delivered in a specific sequence or set pattern. They are spontaneous and delivered in a very intuitive and adaptable manner.*

For reasons of simplicity, I've included a list of *general* probable reaction dynamics your opponent might demonstrate when being razed.

1. He will fall to the ground and curl into a fetal position.

2. He will push you away and attempt to disengage the range.

3. He will rush forward and try to "steam roll" you.

4. He will grab your razing hand and try to pull it off his face.

5. He will turn his head away and expose his back to you.

6. He will swing violently in a futile attempt to get you off of him.

There are other, *more specific,* probable reaction dynamics that might occur when you are razing your adversary. For example:

1. Raking the eyes usually forces the opponent's head down.

2. Palm jolts and vertical elbow strikes often force the opponent's head to snap backwards.

3. Shaving forearms often turn the opponent's head sideways.

4. Short arc hammer fist strikes often bring the opponent's head down.

5. When executing a throat crush, the opponent will almost always attempt to pull your hand away.

Pictured here, a probable reaction dynamic to the palm jolt technique.

Razing techniques are not memorized or delivered in a specific order or set pattern. It's your opponent's reaction dynamics that determine what you will deliver. Therefore, you must be adequately prepared to adapt your razing techniques to every possible reaction dynamic that might occur.

The Razing Stance

Theoretically you can raze your opponent from any standing posture, however if you want to maximize the effectiveness of your assault you should employ razing techniques from a good stance.

A razing stance should function as a *"reference point"* from where you will deliver your offensive strikes while exploiting your opponent's reaction dynamics.

A good stance facilitates optimum execution of your razing techniques while simultaneously protecting your vital body targets against a counter strike.

To achieve the razing stance, position your feet and body at a 45-degree angle from the opponent. This moves your body targets back and away from direct attack but leaves you strategically positioned to raze your adversary.

When assuming a razing stance, place your weak side to the front. For example, a right-handed person stands with his or her left side toward the assailant. Keeping your weakest side to the front enhances the stability of your anchor while maximizing the power of your razing arm. This doesn't mean that you should never practice fighting from your other side. You must be capable of razing from both sides, and you should spend equal practice time on the left and right stances.

When assuming your razing stance, place your feet slightly wider than shoulder width apart. Keep your knees bent and flexible. You must be stable when razing your adversary, so keep fifty percent of your body weight on each leg and always be in control of it.

Razing & Anchoring

In Chapter 2, I discussed the various ways you can anchor your opponent. Since we are discussing razing in this chapter, this section just serves as a brief review of offensive anchoring.

Pictured here, the author demonstrates the proper anchoring technique for razing.

As I said earlier, anchoring is the strategic process of trapping the assailant's limb in order to control the range of engagement. Once again, the opponent's neck is the ideal "anchor point" when delivering your razing techniques.

Anchoring is critical for effective razing skills for the following five reasons:

1. It maintains the close quarter range necessary for effective and continuous razing.

2. It prevents the adversary from disengaging from you when you are razing him. In essence, the two of you are "locked up"

until you choose to break the connection.

3. By anchoring the opponent's neck you will maximizes the damage of your razing techniques. It permits you to apply maximum pressure against facial and throat targets.

4. It provides a "tactile" reference point if your vision is impaired during the course of the fight. As a matter of fact, if you are adequately trained, you can perform razing techniques without actually seeing your opponent. Essentially, if you can feel the opponent, you can raze him!

5. Controlling the opponent's neck is a very dominant action that transmits a very strong message to your adversary. Psychologically, the action of anchoring establishes you as an *"Alpha"* or *"Predator."* When this is combined with razing, your opponent immediately becomes psychologically terrorized.

Sometimes you can use your environment to help anchor or stabilize your adversary when razing. For example, you can sandwich your opponent between you and a wall, vending machine, door, tall fence, or automobile.

Razing Limitations

Unfortunately, razing is not the be-all and end-all self-defense solution. Actually, no self-defense technique or methodology is an end in itself. Functional self-defense requires you to possess a wide range of skills, tactics and techniques. Razing does have its limitations and should be seen as just another tool in your self-defense tool box.

What follows is a list of several situations when razing should not be used.

1. ***Non Deadly Force situations*** - As I said earlier, razing can produce serious bodily harm and possible death for your adversary. It is classified as deadly force and must only be used when you are legally justified to use deadly force.

2. ***Pain compliance situation*** - Razing should never be used as an intermediate use-of-force response. It's not designed to be a compliance tool to gain control of your opponent.

3. ***Multiple attacker situations*** - Successfully defending against multiple attackers requires the freedom to hit and move around your opponents. Unfortunately, razing requires you to commit and anchor to one opponent at a time. Essentially, your mobility is temporarily inhibited.

4. ***Knife and Edged Weapon situations*** - The number one rule when defending against an edged weapon attack is to ***always control the weapon first and then neutralize the assailant.*** Razing a knife wielding adversary with one hand while attempting to control his knife with your other is a foolish action that will almost certainly get you killed.

Razing Demonstrations

To give you a better understanding of my razing methodology, I've included nine different razing demonstrations. Keep in mind that all of the following razing sequences are performed and completed in just a few seconds.

About the Photographs

Also, the following photographs were taken during a live razing demonstration. They are snapshots of fast and dynamic movements in real-time. They are not posed!

Unfortunately, still photographs don't do justice to the ferocious nature of razing. To truly appreciate the Widow Maker program and witness how fast and devastating razing can be, I strongly encourage you to watch the numerous razing demonstrations featured in my Widow Maker video. It truly is a sight to behold. You can find it on my website and Amazon.com

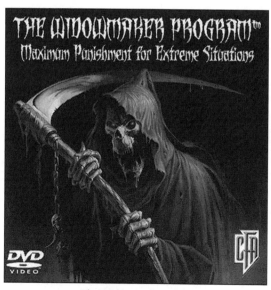

The Widow Maker DVD

Razing Demonstration #1

Step 1: Franco begins with his left hand anchored behind the neck.

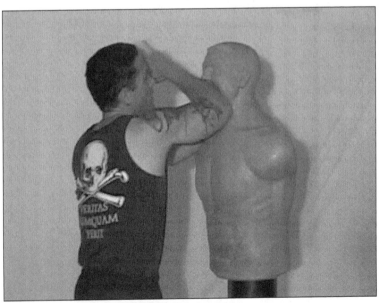

Step 2: The razing begins with a shaving forearm.

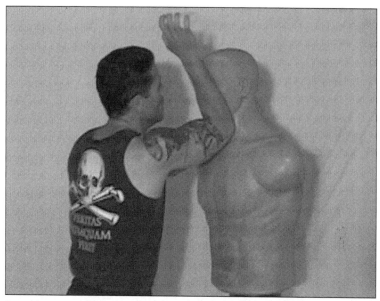

Step 3: As Franco drives his forearm across the face, he prepares for an eye rake.

Step 4: Next, he attacks with a vertical eye rake.

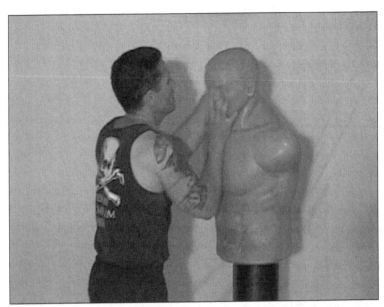

Step 5: As he rakes his hand downward, he prepares for a palm jolt.

Step 6: Franco delivers a palm jolt to the chin.

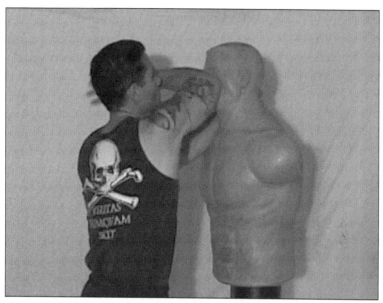

Step 7: Without breaking contact with the face, he delivers a diagonal elbow strike.

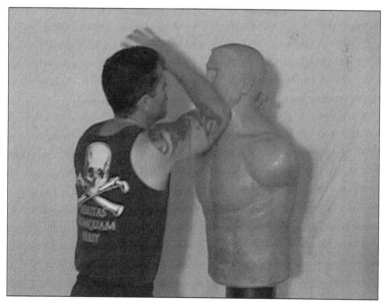

Step 8: After delivering the elbow strike, he attacks with a reverse shaving forearm.

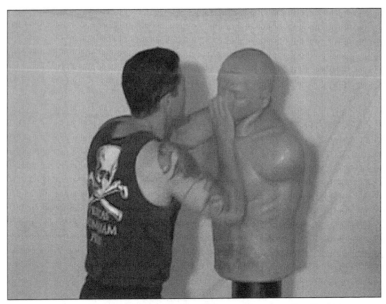

Step 9: The shaving forearm turns into another eye rake attack.

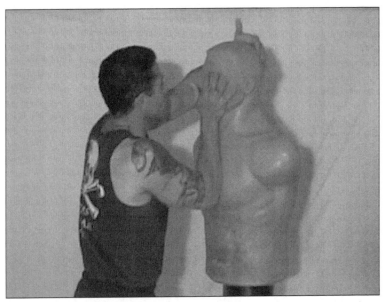

Step 10: Once again, without breaking contact, Franco sets up the neck crank.

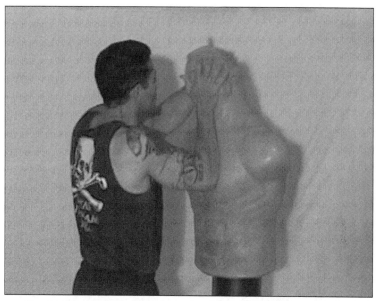

Step 11: Franco cranks the neck counter clockwise with both of his hands.

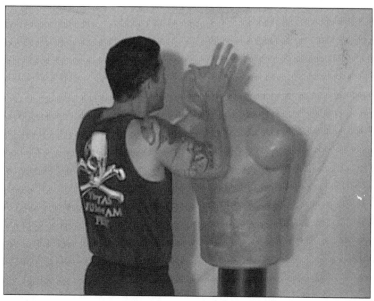

Step 12: The razing sequence is complete.

Razing Demonstration #2

Step 1: Franco begins with his left hand anchoring the neck.

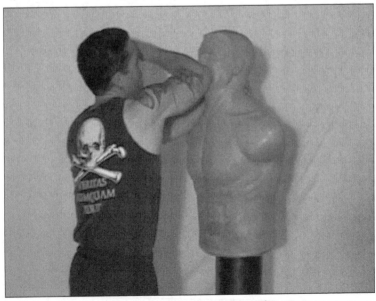

Step 2: The razing begins with a shaving forearm.

Step 3: Franco follows up with a short arc hammer fist strike to the nose.

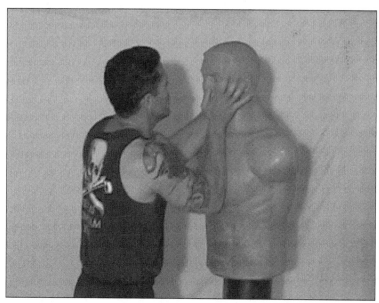

Step 4: Next, he attacks with a palm jolt to the chin.

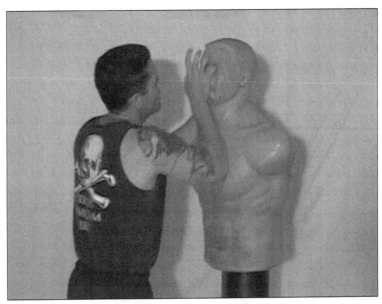

Step 5: He follows up with an eye rake.

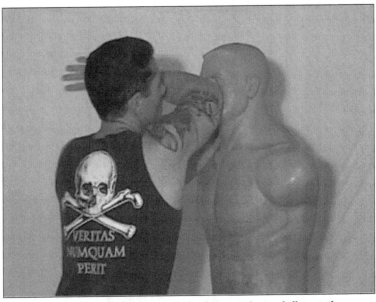

Step 6: Without breaking contact, he delivers a diagonal elbow strike.

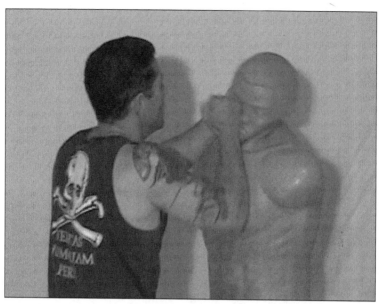

Step 7: Franco attacks with a short arc hammer fist strike to the nose.

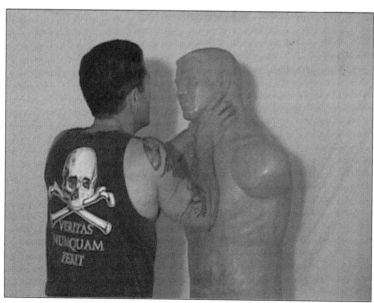

Step 8: The razing sequence is completed with a throat crush.

Razing Demonstration #3

Step 1: Franco begins with his left hand anchoring the neck.

Step 2: The razing begins with an eye rake.

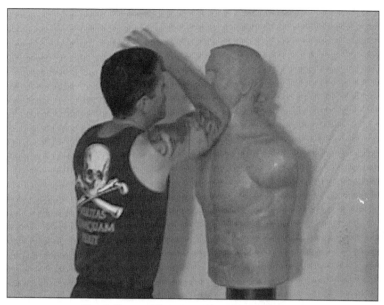

Step 3: Franco follows up with a shaving forearm.

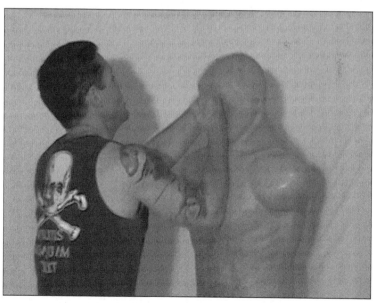

Step 4: Next, he drives a short arc hammer fist to the nose.

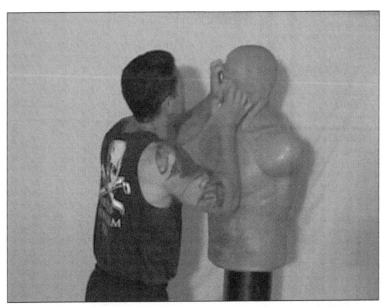

Step 5: Franco releases the anchor from behind the neck and prepares to deliver a double thumb gouge.

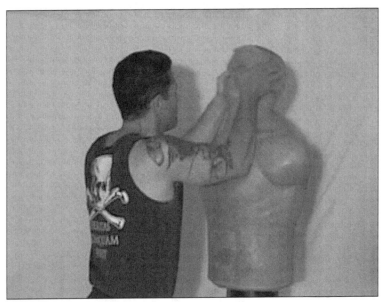

Step 6: The razing sequence ends with a double thumb gouge to the eyes.

Razing Demonstration #4

Step 1: Franco begins with his left hand anchored behind the neck.

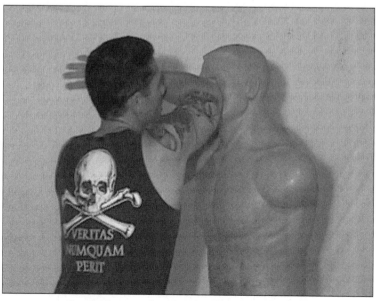

Step 2: The razing begins with a diagonal elbow strike.

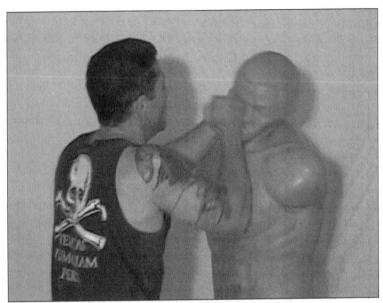

Step 3: Next, Franco follows up with a short arc hammer fist strike.

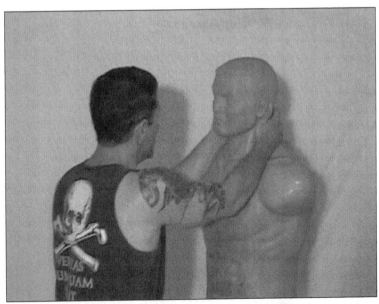

Step 4: Franco grasps the neck with his right hand.

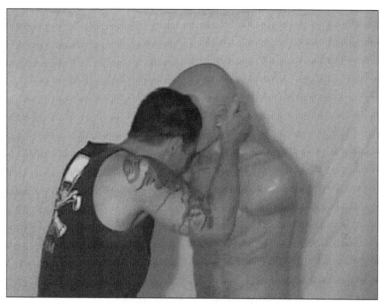

Step 5: He immediately attacks with a head butt to the nose.

Step 6: Franco retracts his head back and prepares to deliver another strike.

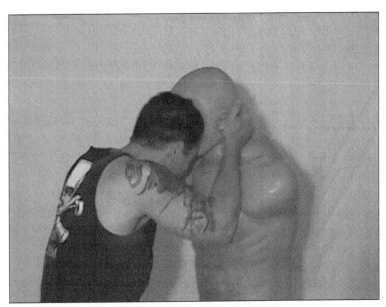

Step 7: He drives another head butt strike.

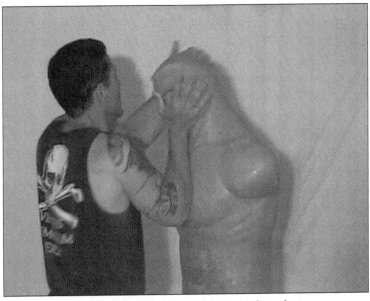

Step 8: Franco prepares to deliver a neck crank.

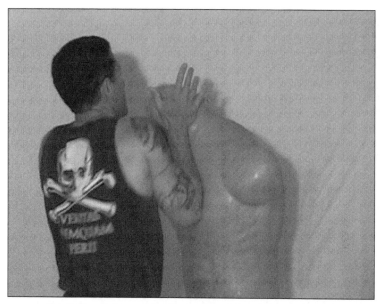

Step 9: The razing sequence is complete with a violent neck crank.

Razing Demonstration #5

Step 1: Franco prepares to raze the bag.

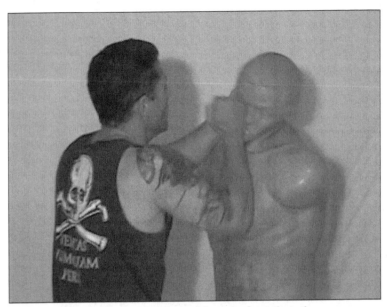

Step 2: He begins with a short arc hammer fist strike to the nose.

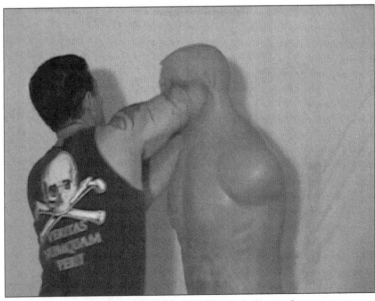

Step 3: He follows up with a diagonal elbow strike.

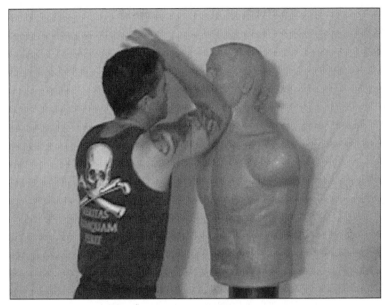

Step 4: Next, a reverse shaving forearm.

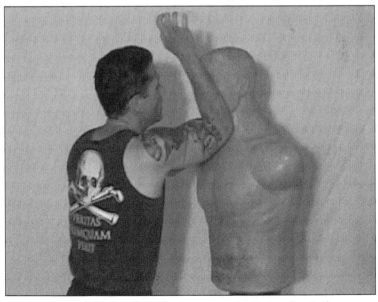

Step 5: As his arm descends, Franco prepares an eye rake attack.

Step 6: Franco rakes his fingers into the eyes of the bag.

Step 7: He releases his left hand from behind the neck.

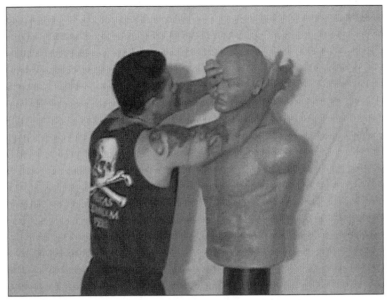

Step 8: And begins razing with his left hand.

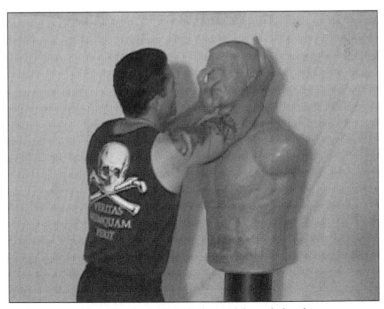

Step 9: Franco anchors the bag with his right hand.

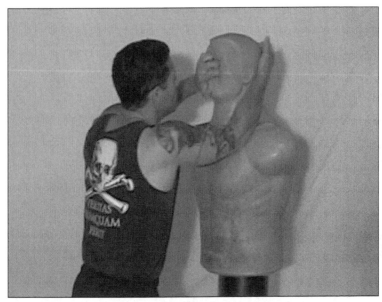

Step 10: Next, he delivers a horizontal eye rake.

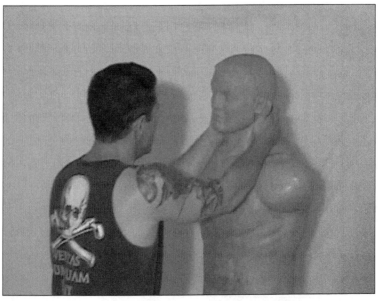

Step 11: Franco grasps the neck with two hands.

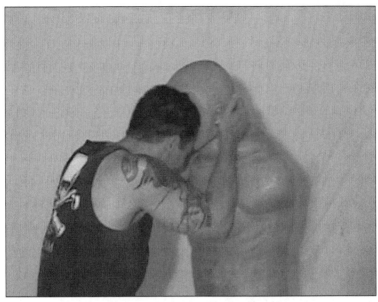

Step 12: He attacks with a head butt strike to the nose.

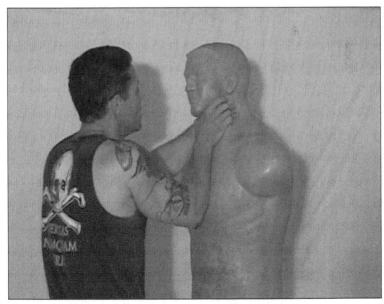

Step 13: The razing sequence is completed with a throat crush.

Razing Demonstration #6

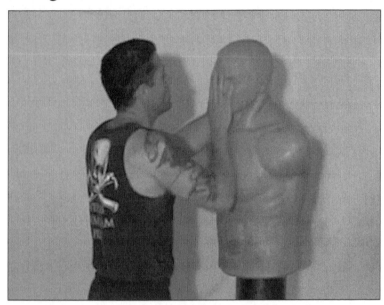

Step 1: Franco begins with his left hand anchoring the neck.

Step 2: He starts with a palm jolt to the chin.

Step 3: Next, he rakes his fingers into the eyes of the bag.

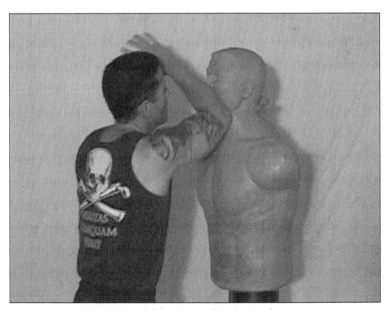

Step 4: Franco follows up with a shaving forearm.

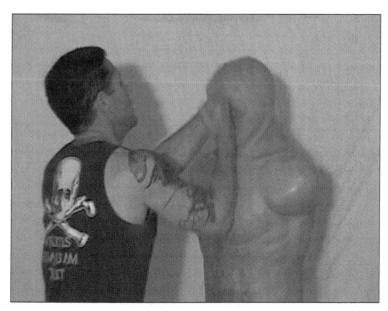

Step 5: He drives a short arc hammer fist to the nose.

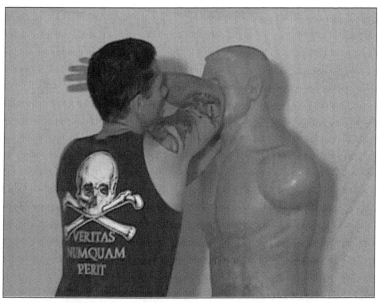

Step 6: Without breaking contact, he delivers a diagonal elbow strike.

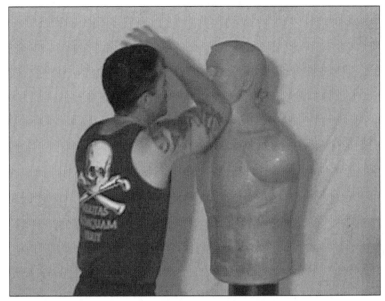

Step 7: Next, a reverse shaving forearm.

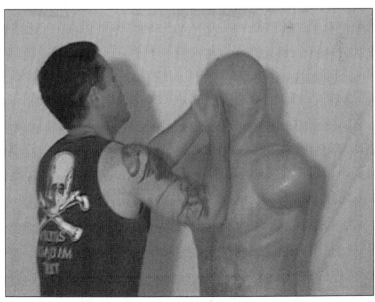

Step 8: The shaving forearm converts into another short arc hammer fist.

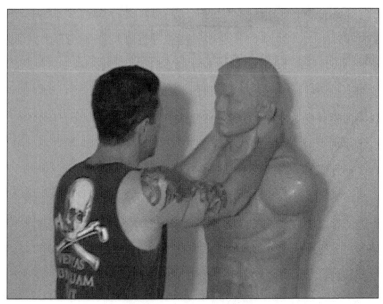

Step 9: Franco grasps the neck with two hands.

Step 10: He attacks with a head butt strike to the nose.

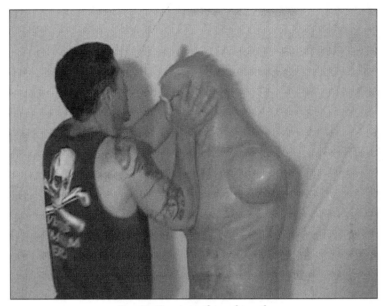

Step 11: He sets up the neck crank.

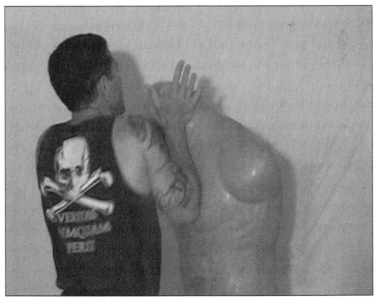

Step 12: The razing sequence ends with a violent neck crank.

Razing Demonstration #7

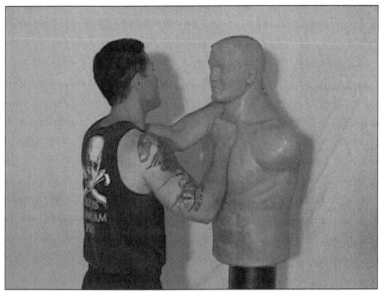

Step 1: Franco begins with his left hand anchoring the neck.

Step 2: He starts with a palm jolt to the chin.

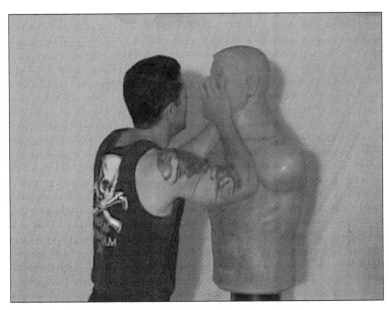

Step 3: Franco rakes his fingers into the eyes of the bag.

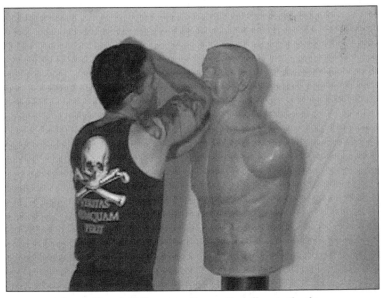

Step 4: Next, he follows up with a vertical elbow to the chin.

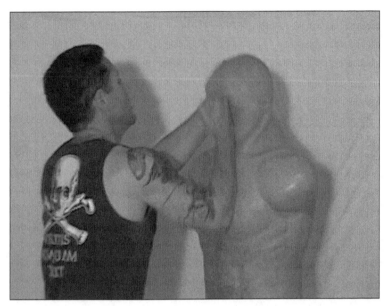

Step 5: Franco continues with a short arc hammer fist to the nose.

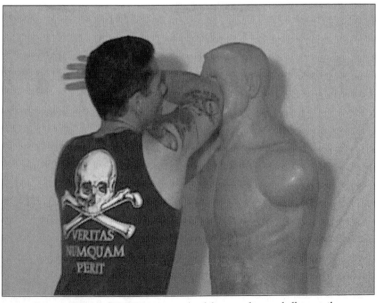

Step 6: Without breaking contact, he delivers a diagonal elbow strike.

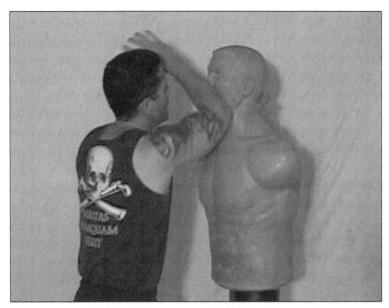

Step 7: Next, a reverse shaving forearm.

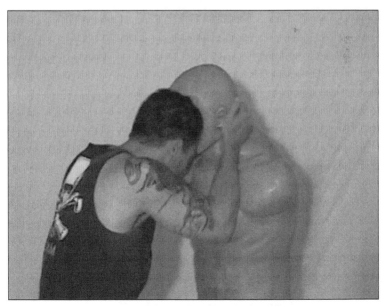

Step 8: He attacks with a head butt strike to the nose.

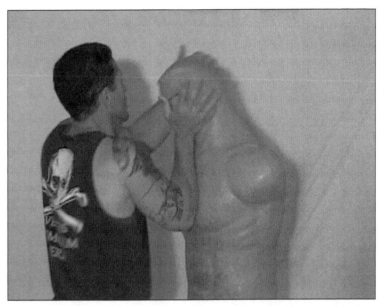

Step 9: Franco sets up the neck crank.

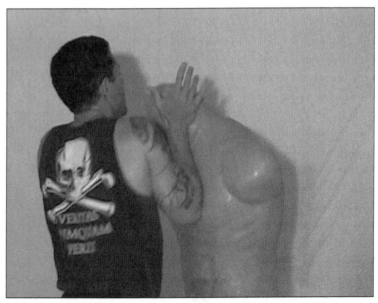

Step 10: The razing sequence is completed with a violent neck crank.

Razing Demonstration #8

Step 1: Franco anchors the back of the neck.

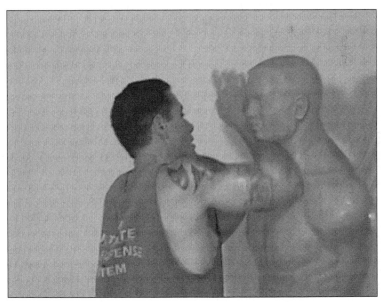

Step 2: He begins with a shaving forearm across the throat.

Step 3: Next, he attacks with a short arc hammer fist strike.

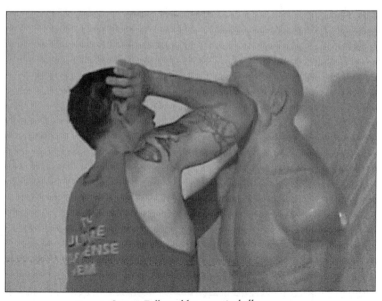

Step 4: Followed by a vertical elbow.

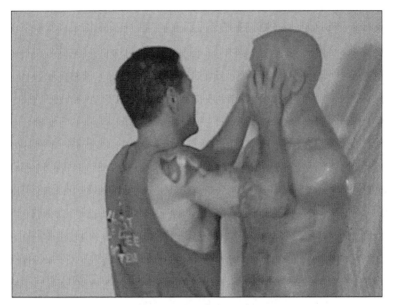

Step 5: Next is the eye rake.

Step 6: He immediately attacks with a shaving forearm across the face.

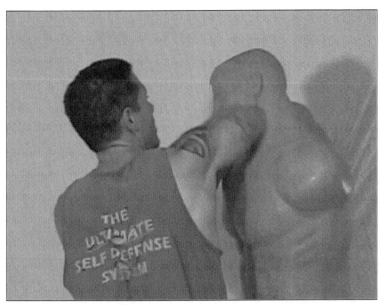

Step 7: The shaving forearm converts to an elbow strike.

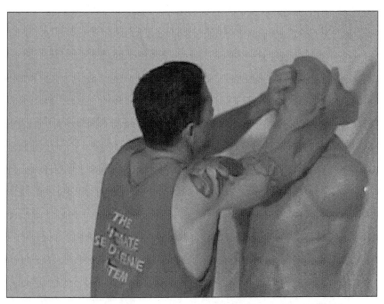

Step 8: Franco switches anchors and rips the nose with his left hand.

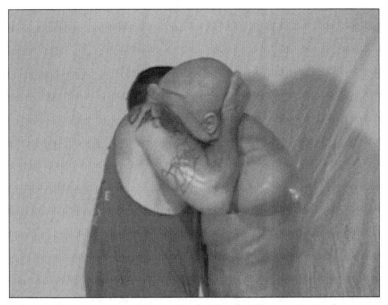

Step 9: The razing sequence is completed with a deep bite into the jugular vein.

When performing razing techniques, remember to breathe. Breathing is one of the most important and often neglected aspects of razing. Proper breathing promotes muscular relaxation and increases the speed and efficiency of your assault.

Razing Demonstration #9

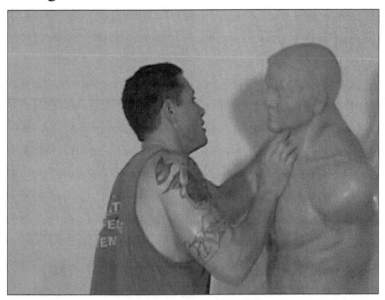

Step 1: Franco anchors the back of the neck.

Step 2: He begins with a short arc hammer fist strike.

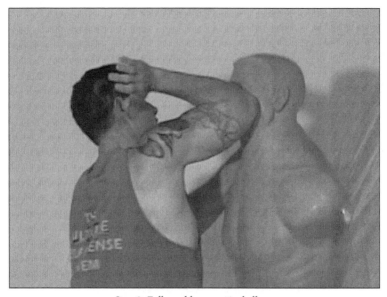

Step 3: Followed by a vertical elbow.

Step 4: He attacks with another short arc hammer fist.

Step 5: He follows up with a shaving forearm across the face.

Step 6: Next, a reverse shaving forearm.

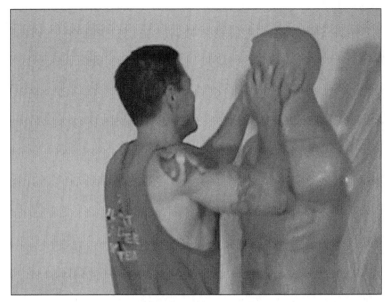

Step 7: Followed by an eye rake.

Step 8: The razing sequence is complete with a deep bite into the jugular vein.

More Razing Tips

Here are some important points to keep in mind when applying razing techniques.

1. Never raze your adversary in a set pattern. Your attack is always predicated on your opponent's reaction dynamics.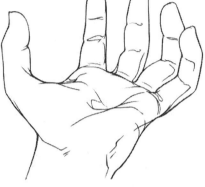

2. Don't "force the raze." Let your series of strikes flow naturally and easily.

3. Always remain relaxed when razing. Tightening your muscles will only slow you down and break your offensive flow.

4. Keep your razing movement tight and clean. Avoid sloppy telegraphic movements.

5. Remember to breathe. Breathing is one of the most important and often neglected aspects of razing. Proper breathing promotes muscular relaxation and increases the speed and efficiency of your assault.

6. Always be mindful of your razing stance. Never stand squarely in front of your assailant when razing. Not only does this expose your body targets, it also diminishes your balance and inhibits footwork. Always try to maintain a forty-five degree stance from your assailant.

7. Avoid switching anchors unless it is absolutely necessary.

8. Always be aware of your environment (especially the terrain) when razing your adversary.

9. Never use your opponent's clothing as an anchor.

10. Avoid using kicking techniques and knee strikes when razing your adversary.

11. Since biting runs the risk of being infected with a variety of diseases, it should only be used as a "last resort" razing technique.

12. Always try to maintain a fifty percent weight distribution when razing your adversary.

13. Have confidence in what you are doing. Remember, action will always beat reaction!

14. Remember that razing is a both a physical and psychological weapon.

15. You don't need long or sharp nails to raze your adversary.

16. Don't overlook the importance of anchoring the opponent's neck. Remember, the structural integrity of your neck anchor often determines the power and effectiveness of your razing techniques.

17. Don't apply razing techniques if you are defending against multiple attackers.

18. Don't apply razing techniques when defending against a knife or edged weapon attack.

19. Never use razing as a pain compliance tactic.

20. Never apply fish-hooking techniques (i.e., inserting fingers in the mouth) when razing your adversary.

21. Never practice razing techniques on a training partner. Someone will get hurt!

22. While razing techniques can be applied in a ground fight, it requires a specialized form of training.

23. Razing skills do not require you to be in great shape. However, keep in mind that your odds of surviving any combat altercation is significantly improved if you are in good physical shape.

24. If you are really serious about mastering razing skills, consider purchasing a body opponent bag (BOB).

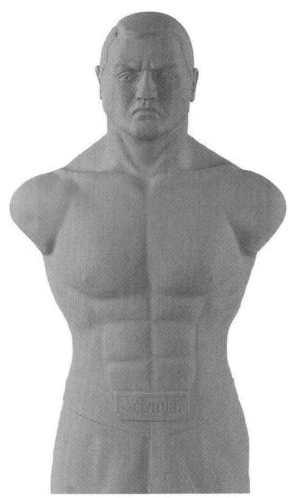

The Body Opponent Bag is the ideal training tool for developing your razing skills. Please see Chapter 4 for more information on razing the body opponent bag.

Chapter Four
Widow Maker Drills & Exercises

In this chapter, I'm going to provide you with a variety of drills and exercises that will help develop and improve your Widow Maker skills. Let's begin with the anchor switching drill.

Anchor Switching Drill

As I discussed in Chapter 2, there might be circumstances when your opponent grabs your razing hand and pulls it away from his face. In such a situation, you will need to switch anchors in order to resume your razing assault. The following sequence of photos demonstrate the anchor switching drill.

Step 1: Franco begins the drill by anchoring his opponents neck with his left hand.

Step 2: Franco begins his razing assault with a palm jolt.

Step 3: Next, he follows up with a shaving forearm.

Step 4: Franco delivers an eye rake.

Step 5: Franco's training partner grabs his right wrist.

Step 6: Next, he traps Franco's right hand to his chest.

Step 7: The training partner releases Franco's left hand. Franco resumes razing.

Step 8: Franco delivers a Palm jolt.

Step 9: He follows up with an eye rake.

Step 10: Franco drags the eye rake downward.

Step 11: Next, he applies a shaving forearm.

Step 12: The training partner grabs Franco's left wrist.

Step 13: Next, he releases Franco's right hand. Franco resumes razing.

Step 14: Franco continues his assault until his training partner grabs his wrist.

Anchor Switching Limitations

Since the anchor switching drill requires you to perform razing skills on your live training partner, you must be especially careful with the speed and intensity of the assault. You might find a training partner that is overly sensitive to certain targets. The following photos demonstrate how your training partner might reflexively disengage from the drill.

Here, Franco performs the anchor switching drill with his partner.

He attacks his training partner's neck.

Franco's training partner reflexively disengages from the drill.

To remedy the problem, Franco uses a second man to prevent his training partner from disengaging the range of the drill.

Controlled Widow Maker Simulations

If you are well versed in the Widow Maker techniques and have a solid understanding of safety and control, you can perform both webbing and razing simulations. Once again, this drill should only be performed by practitioners who possess an exceptional amount of control.

Step 1: The simulation begins with Franco (right) assuming a first strike stance.

Warning! Widow Maker simulations must always be perform in a very slow and controlled manner. Never deliver full speed, full force techniques on your training partner.

Step 2: His training partner rushes forward and Franco intercepts him with a controlled webbing strike to the chin.

Step 3: Once contact is made, Franco anchors his partner's neck with his left hand.

Step 4: Franco delivers a shaving forearm.

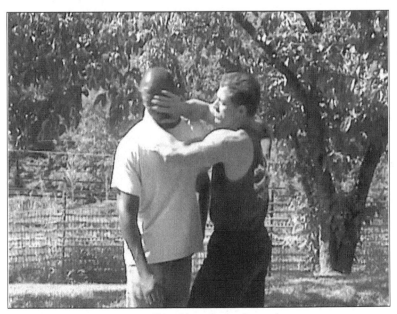

Step 5: Followed by a diagonal eye rake.

Step 6: Next, in a slow and controlled fashion, Franco performs the neck crank technique.

Step 7: Franco carefully turns his training partner's neck counter clockwise.

Step 8: Franco's partner finds himself in a rear naked choke hold.

Step 9: Once the choke is solidified, Franco takes his training partner to the ground.

The Insertion Drill

This simple exercise develops tactile sensitivity for locating facial gaps and openings when razing your opponent. To avoid injuries, the insertion drill is applied to your training partners hands, not his face. Depending on your skill level, this drill can also be performed with your eyes open or closed.

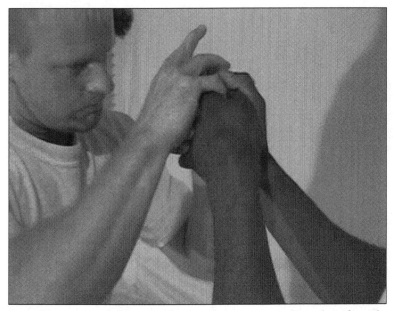

Step 1: The insertion drill begins with your training partner making a large fist with both hands.

Not only does the Insertion drill develop tactile sensitivity, it also strengthens your hands and fingers for the rigors of full-force razing.

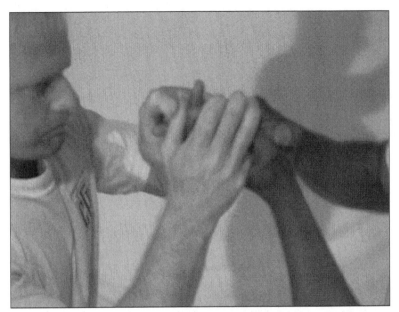

Step 2: Begin the drill by placing both of your hands over your training partner's fist.

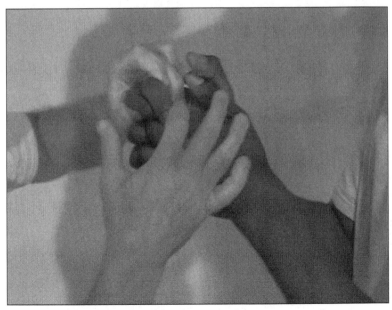

Step 3: Next, start inserting your fingers into the various gaps and opening.

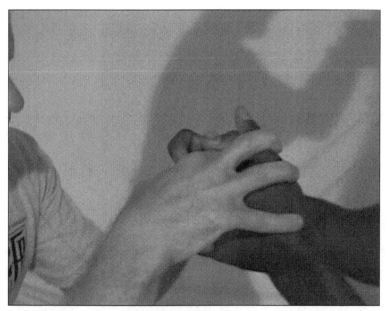

Step 4: Take your time and work each of your fingers into the different openings.

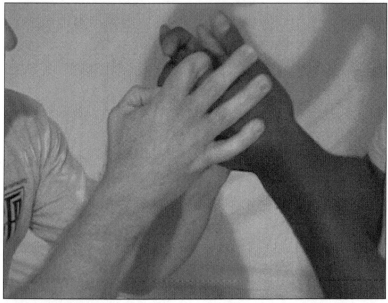

Note: Your training partner controls the level of difficulty by how hard he compresses his hands together.

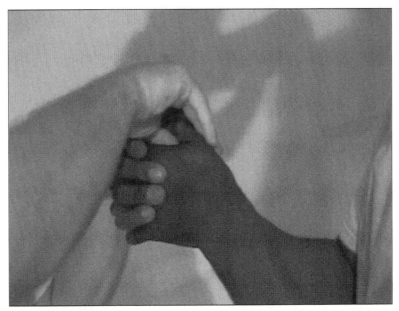

Step 5: Your training partner can also randomly adjust the hight of his arms while your are performing the drill.

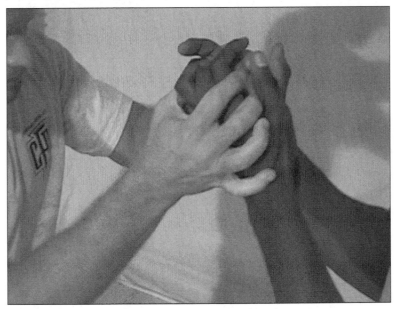

Step 6: Finally, your partner can step forward and backward, requiring you to maintain the proper razing distance.

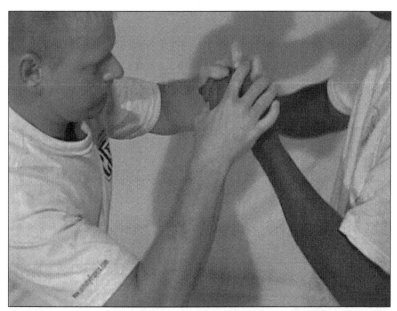

Step 7: Perform the insertion drill for a duration of one minute and then switch with your partner.

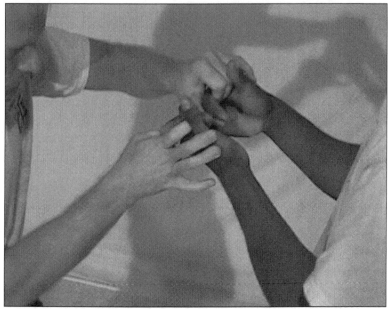

Pictured here, a common mistake is for your training partner's fist to break open during the drill.

Razing the Body Opponent Bag

The body opponent bag (aka BOB) is, by far, the best piece of training equipment for developing your razing skills and techniques. Unlike the traditional heavy bag, this freestanding mannequin bag provides realistic facial targets that you can attack with full-speed, full-force strikes.

Effective razing skills take time and practice to master. Remember to start out slowly and progressively build up the speed and intensity of your quarter beat strikes. If you are a beginner, avoid the urge to attack the bag with maximum speed and force. Take your time and enjoy the process of learning a new skill.

What follows is a list of tips to help maximize your razing skills when training on the body opponent bag.

While the heavy bag is a tried-and-true piece of training equipment, it's practically useless for developing razing skills.

Tips for Razing the Body Opponent Bag

Here are ten important points to keep in mind when razing the body opponent bag.

1. Don't "force the raze". Let your series of strikes flow naturally and easily.

2. Don't forget to include biting tactics in your training.

3. Always remain relaxed when razing. Tightening your muscles will only slow you down and break your offensive flow.

4. Get into the habit of executing "zero beat" techniques at the end of your razing combination.

5. Practice your razing skills at least three times per week (30 minutes per workout session) for six consecutive months.

6. Keep your razing movement "clean" and "tight", avoid sloppy telegraphic movements.

7. While the body opponent bag is a useful training tool, understand and recognize its inherent limitations. Remember, razing a stationary mannequin bag is nothing like razing an adrenaline induced human being.

8. If you want to improve the speed and overall flow of your razing techniques during your workout, you can apply petroleum jelly to the BOB's face.

9. Never stand squarely in front of the bag when razing. Not only does this expose vital targets, it also diminishes your balance and inhibits your footwork. Always try to maintain a forty-five degree stance from your assailant.

10. Practice razing with both your weak and dominant hands.

Body Opponent Bag Targets

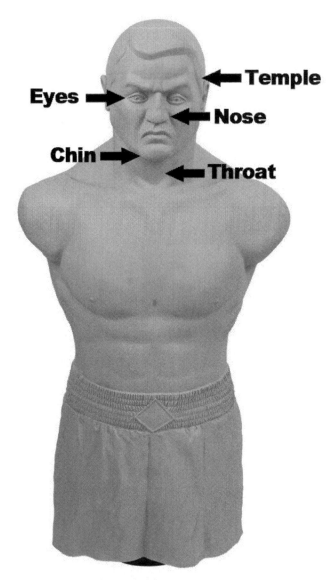

The primary razing targets on the body opponent bag include: the temple, eyes, nose, chin, and throat.

Right Hand Razing Combinations

The following ten razing combinations should be performed with your right hand while anchoring the neck with your left.

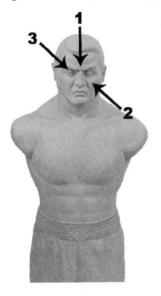

Razing Combination #1

1. Eye Rake
2. Shaving Forearm
3. Hammer Fist Strike

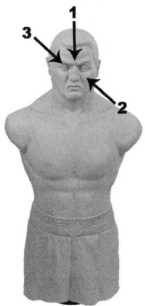

Razing Combination #2

1. Short Arc Hammer Fist
2. Diagonal Elbow
3. Diagonal Eye Rake

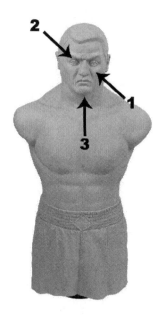

Razing Combination #3

1. Shaving Forearm
2. Reverse Shaving Forearm
3. Palm Jolt

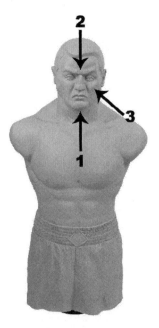

Razing Combination #4

1. Palm Jolt
2. Eye Rake
3. Shaving Forearm

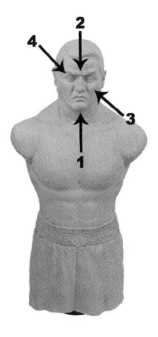

Razing Combination #5

1. Vertical Elbow

2. Short Arc Hammer Fist

3. Shaving Forearm

4. Diagonal Eye Rake

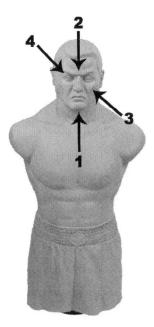

Razing Combination #6

1. Palm Jolt

2. Short Arc Hammer Fist

3. Shaving Forearm

4. Reverse Shaving Forearm

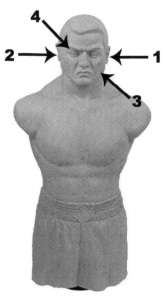

Razing Combination #7

1. Horizontal Elbow
2. Shaving Forearm
3. Shaving Forearm
4. Short Arc Hammer Fist

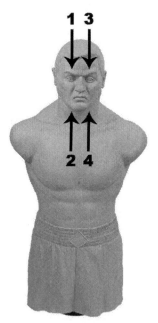

Razing Combination #8

1. Eye Rake
2. Palm Jolt
3. Eye Rake
4. Palm Jolt

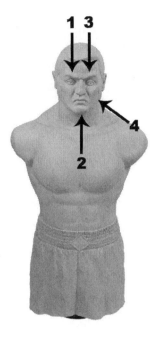

Razing Combination #9

1. Short Arc Hammer Fist
2. Vertical Elbow
3. Eye Rake
4. Shaving Forearm

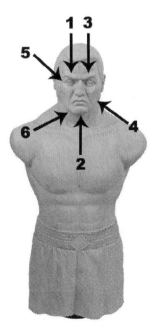

Razing Combination #10

1. Eye Rake
2. Vertical Elbow
3. Short Arc Hammer Fist
4. Shaving Forearm
5. Reverse Shaving Forearm
6. Neck Crank

The Widow Maker Program

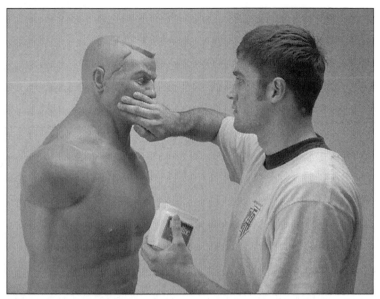

If you want to improve the speed of your razing techniques during your workout, you can apply petroleum jelly to the BOB's face.

Warning! If you are new to razing, be very careful when working on the body opponent bag. If you are not careful, you can tear or sprain your fingers. Remember to take your time and progressively build up the intensity of your workouts.

Left Hand Razing Combinations

The following ten razing combinations should be performed with your left hand while anchoring the neck with your right.

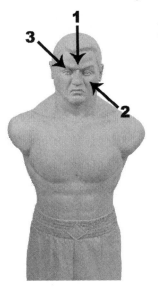

Razing Combination #1

1. Eye Rake
2. Shaving Forearm
3. Hammer Fist Strike

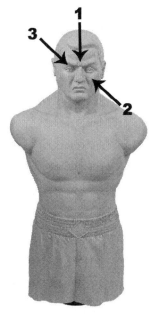

Razing Combination #2

1. Short Arc Hammer Fist
2. Diagonal Elbow
3. Diagonal Eye Rake

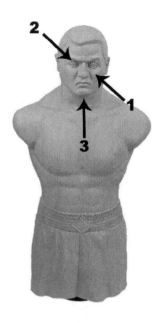

Razing Combination #3

1. Shaving Forearm
2. Reverse Shaving Forearm
3. Palm Jolt

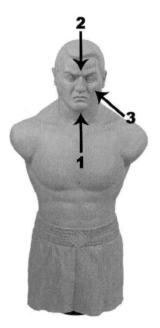

Razing Combination #4

1. Palm Jolt
2. Eye Rake
3. Shaving Forearm

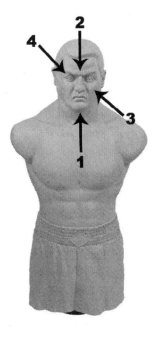

Razing Combination #5

1. Vertical Elbow
2. Short Arc Hammer Fist
3. Shaving Forearm
4. Diagonal Eye Rake

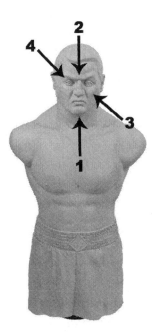

Razing Combination #6

1. Palm Jolt
2. Short Arc Hammer Fist
3. Shaving Forearm
4. Reverse Shaving Forearm

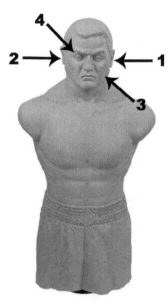

Razing Combination #7

1. Horizontal Elbow
2. Shaving Forearm
3. Shaving Forearm
4. Short Arc Hammer Fist

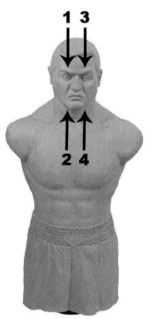

Razing Combination #8

1. Eye Rake
2. Palm Jolt
3. Eye Rake
4. Palm Jolt

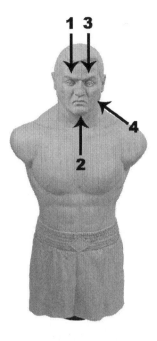

Razing Combination #9

1. Short Arc Hammer Fist
2. Vertical Elbow
3. Eye Rake
4. Shaving Forearm

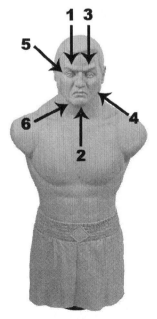

Razing Combination #10

1. Eye Rake
2. Vertical Elbow
3. Short Arc Hammer Fist
4. Shaving Forearm
5. Reverse Shaving Forearm
6. Neck Crank

he Widow Maker Program

Create Your Own Razing Combinations

Use this section to write down your own razing combinations.

1.

2.

3.

4.

5.

6.

7.

8.

9.

10.

11.

12.

13.

14.

15.

16.

17.

18.

19.

29.

21.

22.

23.

24.

25.

26.

27.

28.

29.

30.

31.

32.

33.

34.

35.

36.

37.

38.

39.

40.

Widow Maker Conditioning

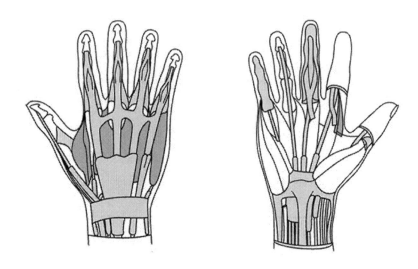

Fingers, Hands, Wrists & Forearms

It's no surprise that strong fingers, wrists and forearms will significantly enhance your razing skills. Powerful hands and forearms will amplify the power of your rakes, gouges, and tearing techniques. Strong forearms will enhance techniques such as neck cranks, rear naked chokes, and anchoring. There are several effective hand and forearm exercises you can perform to strengthen these muscles.

What follows are several ways to condition and strengthen your hands, wrists and forearms.

Power Putty

One excellent hand exerciser that strengthens all the muscles in your fingers and hands is Power Putty. Essentially, Power Putty is a flexible silicone rubber that can be squeezed, stretched, and crushed. Begin using the putty for ten minute sessions and progressively build up to thirty minutes.

This tough resistant putty will strengthen the muscles of your forearm, wrists, hands and fingers. Remember to work both hands equally.

Power Putty is ideal for hand conditioning.

Hand Grippers

Another effective way to strengthen your hands, wrists and forearms is to work out with heavy duty hand grippers. While there are a wide selection of them on the market, I personally prefer using the Captains of Crush brand. These high quality grippers are virtually indestructible and they are sold in a variety of different resistance levels ranging from 60 to 365 pounds.

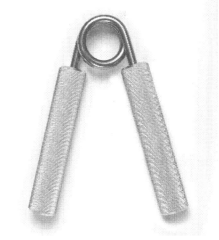

Captains of Crush hand grippers are the best on the market!

Tennis Ball

If you are low on cash and just starting out with your training, you can begin by squeezing a tennis ball a couple times per week. One hundred repetitions per hand would be a great start.

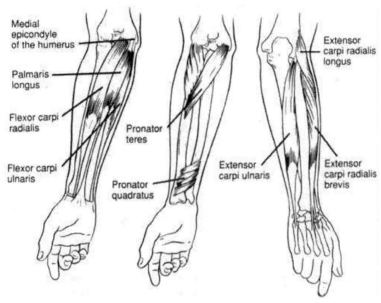

Anatomy of the human forearm.

Weight Training

Finally, you can also condition your wrists and forearms by performing various forearm exercises with free weights. Exercises like: hammer curls, reverse curls, wrist curls, and reverse wrist curls are great for developing powerful forearms. When training your forearms, be certain to work both your extensor and flexor muscles. Let's look at some of the exercises.

Barbell Wrist Curls

This exercise strengthens the flexor muscles. Perform 5 sets of 8-10 repetitions. To perform the exercise, follow these steps:

1. Sit at the end of a bench, grab a barbell with an underhand grip and place both of your hands close together.

2. In a smooth and controlled fashion, slowly bend your wrists and lower the barbell toward the floor.

3. Contract your forearms and curl the weight back to the starting position.

Reverse Wrist Curls

This exercise develops and strengthens the extensor muscle of the forearm. Perform 6 sets of 6-8 repetitions. To perform the exercise, follow these steps:

1. Sit at the end of a bench, hold a barbell with an overhand grip (your hands should be approximately 11 inches apart) and place your forearms on top of your thighs.

2. Slowly lower the barbell as far as your wrists will allow.

3. Flex your wrists upward back to the starting position.

Behind-the-Back Wrist Curls

This exercise strengthens both the flexor muscles of the forearms. Perform 5 sets of 6-8 repetitions To perform the exercise, follow these steps:

1. Hold a barbell behind your back at arm's length (your hands should be approximately shoulder-width apart).

2. Uncurl your finger and let the barbell slowly roll down your palms.

3. Close your hands and roll the barbell back into your hands.

Free weights are one of the best ways to strengthen your forearms.

Hammer Curls

This exercise strengthens both the Brachialis and Brachioradialis muscles. Perform 5 sets of 8-10 repetitions. To perform the exercise, follow these steps:

1. Stand with both feet approximately shoulder width apart, with both dumbbells at your sides.

2. Keeping your elbows close to your body and your palms facing inward, slowly curl both dumbbells upward towards your shoulders.

3. Slowly return to the starting position.

Reverse Barbell Curls

Reverse curls can be a great alternative to hammer curls. This exercise strengthens both the Brachialis and Brachioradialis muscles. Perform 5 sets of 8-10 repetitions. To perform the exercise, follow these steps:

1. Stand with both feet approximately shoulder width apart. Hold a barbell with your palms facing down (pronated grip).

2. Keeping your upper arms stationary, curl the weights up until the bar is at shoulder level.

3. Slowly return to the starting position.

*Conditioning and training should not be limited to your hands and forearms. Consider adding a complete combat conditioning program to your training regimen. For more information, check out **War Machine: How to Transform Yourself Into a Vicious and Deadly Street Fighter***

The Widow Maker Program

More Widow Maker Resources

Widow Maker Video

As I mentioned in Chapter 3, still photographs don't do justice to the overwhelming and destructive nature of razing. To truly appreciate the Widow Maker program and witness how fast and devastating razing can be, I encourage you to watch the numerous razing demonstrations featured in my Widow Maker video. It truly is a sight to behold.

The Widow Maker Program DVD

Feral Fighting: Advanced Widow Maker Techniques

Believe it or not, this book just scratches the surface of the Widow Maker program. There are many more advanced concepts and techniques to this unique and revolutionary method of unarmed combat. Some advanced techniques include:

- **The Shielding Wedge**

The Widow Maker Program

- The Jersey Pull
- The Neck Crush
- The Trap and Tuck
- Sharking
- Scorching

So for those of you who would like to take the Widow Maker Program to the next level, be sure to look into *Feral Fighting: Advanced Widow Maker Techniques.*

Feral Fighting DVD

Glossary

The following terms are defined in the context of Contemporary Fighting Arts and its related concepts. In many instances, the definitions bear little resemblance to those found in a standard dictionary.

A

accuracy—The precise or exact projection of force. Accuracy is also defined as the ability to execute a combative movement with precision and exactness.

adaptability—The ability to physically and psychologically adjust to new or different conditions or circumstances of combat.

advanced first-strike tools—Offensive techniques that are specifically used when confronted with multiple opponents.

aerobic exercise—Literally, "with air." Exercise that elevates the heart rate to a training level for a prolonged period of time, usually 30 minutes.

affective preparedness – One of the three components of preparedness. Affective preparedness means being emotionally, philosophically, and spiritually prepared for the strains of combat. See cognitive preparedness and psychomotor preparedness.

aggression—Hostile and injurious behavior directed toward a person.

aggressive response—One of the three possible counters when assaulted by a grab, choke, or hold from a standing position. Aggressive response requires you to counter the enemy with destructive blows and strikes. See moderate response and passive response.

aggressive hand positioning—Placement of hands so as to imply aggressive or hostile intentions.

agility—An attribute of combat. One's ability to move his or her body quickly and gracefully.

amalgamation—A scientific process of uniting or merging.

ambidextrous—The ability to perform with equal facility on both the right and left sides of the body.

anabolic steroids – synthetic chemical compounds that resemble the male sex hormone testosterone. This performance-enhancing drug is known to increase lean muscle mass, strength, and endurance.

analysis and integration—One of the five elements of CFA's mental component. This is the painstaking process of breaking down various elements, concepts, sciences, and disciplines into their atomic parts, and then methodically and strategically analyzing, experimenting, and drastically modifying the information so that it fulfills three combative requirements: efficiency, effectiveness, and safety. Only then is it finally integrated into the CFA system.

anatomical striking targets—The various anatomical body targets that can be struck and which are especially vulnerable to potential harm. They include: the eyes, temple, nose, chin, back of neck, front of neck, solar plexus, ribs, groin, thighs, knees, shins, and instep.

anchoring – The strategic process of trapping the assailant's neck or limb in order to control the range of engagement during razing.

assailant—A person who threatens or attacks another person.

assault—The threat or willful attempt to inflict injury upon the person of another.

assault and battery—The unlawful touching of another person without justification.

assessment—The process of rapidly gathering, analyzing, and accurately evaluating information in terms of threat and danger. You can assess people, places, actions, and objects.

attack—Offensive action designed to physically control, injure, or kill another person.

attitude—One of the three factors that determine who wins a street fight. Attitude means being emotionally, philosophically, and spiritually liberated from societal and religious mores. See skills and knowledge.

attributes of combat—The physical, mental, and spiritual qualities that enhance combat skills and tactics.

awareness—Perception or knowledge of people, places, actions, and objects. (In CFA, there are three categories of tactical awareness: criminal awareness, situational awareness, and self-awareness.)

B

balance—One's ability to maintain equilibrium while stationary or moving.

blading the body—Strategically positioning your body at a 45-degree angle.

blitz and disengage—A style of sparring whereby a fighter moves into a range of combat, unleashes a strategic compound attack, and then quickly disengages to a safe distance. Of all sparring methodologies, the blitz and disengage most closely resembles a real street fight.

block—A defensive tool designed to intercept the assailant's attack by placing a non-vital target between the assailant's strike and your vital body target.

body composition—The ratio of fat to lean body tissue.

body language—Nonverbal communication through posture, gestures, and facial expressions.

body mechanics—Technically precise body movement during the execution of a body weapon, defensive technique, or other fighting maneuver.

body tackle – A tackle that occurs when your opponent haphazardly rushes forward and plows his body into yours.

body weapon—Also known as a tool, one of the various body parts that can be used to strike or otherwise injure or kill a criminal assailant.

burn out—A negative emotional state acquired by physically over- training. Some symptoms include: illness, boredom, anxiety, disinterest in training, and general sluggishness.

C

cadence—Coordinating tempo and rhythm to establish a timing pattern of movement.

cardiorespiratory conditioning—The component of physical fitness that deals with the heart, lungs, and circulatory system.

centerline—An imaginary vertical line that divides your body in half and which contains many of your vital anatomical targets.

choke holds—Holds that impair the flow of blood or oxygen to the brain.

circular movements—Movements that follow the direction of a curve.

close-quarter combat—One of the three ranges of knife and bludgeon combat. At this distance, you can strike, slash, or stab your assailant with a variety of close-quarter techniques.

cognitive development—One of the five elements of CFA's mental component. The process of developing and enhancing your fighting skills through specific mental exercises and techniques. See analysis and integration, killer instinct, philosophy, and strategic/tactical development.

cognitive exercises—Various mental exercises used to enhance fighting skills and tactics.

cognitive preparedness – One of the three components of preparedness. Cognitive preparedness means being equipped with the strategic concepts, principles, and general knowledge of combat. See affective preparedness and psychomotor preparedness.

combat-oriented training—Training that is specifically related to the harsh realities of both armed and unarmed combat. See ritual-oriented training and sport-oriented training.

combative arts—The various arts of war. See martial arts.

combative attributes—See attributes of combat.

combative fitness—A state characterized by cardiorespiratory and muscular/skeletal conditioning, as well as proper body composition.

combative mentality—Also known as the killer instinct, this is a combative state of mind necessary for fighting. See killer instinct.

combat ranges—The various ranges of unarmed combat.

combative utility—The quality of condition of being combatively useful.

combination(s)—See compound attack.

common peroneal nerve—A pressure point area located approximately four to six inches above the knee on the midline of the outside of the thigh.

composure—A combative attribute. Composure is a quiet and focused mind-set that enables you to acquire your combative agenda.

compound attack—One of the five conventional methods of attack. Two or more body weapons launched in strategic succession whereby the fighter overwhelms his assailant with a flurry of full speed, full-force blows.

conditioning training—A CFA training methodology requiring the practitioner to deliver a variety of offensive and defensive combinations for a 4-minute period. See proficiency training and street training.

contact evasion—Physically moving or manipulating your body to avoid being tackled by the adversary.

Contemporary Fighting Arts—A modern martial art and self-defense system made up of three parts: physical, mental, and spiritual.

conventional ground-fighting tools—Specific ground-fighting techniques designed to control, restrain, and temporarily incapacitate your adversary. Some conventional ground fighting tactics include: submission holds, locks, certain choking techniques, and specific striking techniques.

coordination—A physical attribute characterized by the ability to perform a technique or movement with efficiency, balance, and accuracy.

counterattack—Offensive action made to counter an assailant's initial attack.

courage—A combative attribute. The state of mind and spirit that enables a fighter to face danger and vicissitudes with confidence, resolution, and bravery.

creatine monohydrate—A tasteless and odorless white powder that mimics some of the effects of anabolic steroids. Creatine is a safe body-building product that can benefit anyone who wants to increase their strength, endurance, and lean muscle mass.

criminal awareness—One of the three categories of CFA awareness. It involves a general understanding and knowledge of the nature and dynamics of a criminal's motivations, mentalities, methods, and capabilities to perpetrate violent crime. See situational awareness and self-awareness.

criminal justice—The study of criminal law and the procedures associated with its enforcement.

criminology—The scientific study of crime and criminals.

cross-stepping—The process of crossing one foot in front of or behind the other when moving.

crushing tactics—Nuclear grappling-range techniques designed to crush the assailant's anatomical targets.

D

deadly force—Weapons or techniques that may result in unconsciousness, permanent disfigurement, or death.

deception—A combative attribute. A stratagem whereby you delude your assailant.

decisiveness—A combative attribute. The ability to follow a tactical course of action that is unwavering and focused.

defense—The ability to strategically thwart an assailant's attack (armed or unarmed).

defensive flow—A progression of continuous defensive responses.

defensive mentality—A defensive mind-set.

defensive reaction time—The elapsed time between an assailant's physical attack and your defensive response to that attack. See offensive reaction time.

demeanor—A person's outward behavior. One of the essential factors to consider when assessing a threatening individual.

diet—A lifestyle of healthy eating.

disingenuous vocalization—The strategic and deceptive utilization of words to successfully launch a preemptive strike at your adversary.

distancing—The ability to quickly understand spatial relationships and how they relate to combat.

distractionary tactics—Various verbal and physical tactics designed to distract your adversary.

double-end bag—A small leather ball hung from the ceiling and anchored to the floor with bungee cord. It helps develop striking accuracy, speed, timing, eye-hand coordination, footwork and overall defensive skills.

double-leg takedown—A takedown that occurs when your opponent shoots for both of your legs to force you to the ground.

E

ectomorph—One of the three somatotypes. A body type characterized by a high degree of slenderness, angularity, and fragility. See endomorph and mesomorph.

effectiveness—One of the three criteria for a CFA body weapon, technique, tactic, or maneuver. It means the ability to produce a desired effect. See efficiency and safety.

efficiency—One of the three criteria for a CFA body weapon, technique, tactic, or maneuver. It means the ability to reach an objective quickly and economically. See effectiveness and safety.

emotionless—A combative attribute. Being temporarily devoid of human feeling.

endomorph—One of the three somatotypes. A body type characterized by a high degree of roundness, softness, and body fat. See ectomorph and mesomorph.

evasion—A defensive maneuver that allows you to strategically maneuver your body away from the assailant's strike.

evasive sidestepping—Evasive footwork where the practitioner moves to either the right or left side.

evasiveness—A combative attribute. The ability to avoid threat or danger.

excessive force—An amount of force that exceeds the need for a particular event and is unjustified in the eyes of the law.

experimentation—The painstaking process of testing a combative hypothesis or theory.

explosiveness—A combative attribute that is characterized by a sudden outburst of violent energy.

F

fear—A strong and unpleasant emotion caused by the anticipation or awareness of threat or danger. There are three stages of fear in order of intensity: fright, panic, and terror. See fright, panic, and terror.

feeder—A skilled technician who manipulates the focus mitts.

femoral nerve—A pressure point area located approximately 6 inches above the knee on the inside of the thigh.

fighting stance—Any one of the stances used in CFA's system. A strategic posture you can assume when face-to-face with an unarmed assailant(s). The fighting stance is generally used after you have launched your first-strike tool.

fight-or-flight syndrome—A response of the sympathetic nervous system to a fearful and threatening situation, during which it prepares your body to either fight or flee from the perceived danger.

finesse—A combative attribute. The ability to skillfully execute a movement or a series of movements with grace and refinement.

first strike—Proactive force used to interrupt the initial stages of an assault before it becomes a self-defense situation.

first-strike principle—A CFA principle that states that when physical danger is imminent and you have no other tactical option but to fight back, you should strike first, strike fast, and strike with authority and keep the pressure on.

first-strike stance—One of the stances used in CFA's system. A strategic posture used prior to initiating a first strike.

first-strike tools—Specific offensive tools designed to initiate a preemptive strike against your adversary.

fisted blows – Hand blows delivered with a clenched fist.

five tactical options – The five strategic responses you can make in a self-defense situation, listed in order of increasing level of resistance: comply, escape, de-escalate, assert, and fight back.

flexibility—The muscles' ability to move through maximum natural ranges. See muscular/skeletal conditioning.

focus mitts—Durable leather hand mitts used to develop and sharpen offensive and defensive skills.

footwork—Quick, economical steps performed on the balls of the feet while you are relaxed, alert, and balanced. Footwork is structured around four general movements: forward, backward, right, and left.

fractal tool—Offensive or defensive tools that can be used in more than one combat range.

fright—The first stage of fear; quick and sudden fear. See panic and terror.

full Beat – One of the four beat classifications in the Widow Maker Program. The full beat strike has a complete initiation and retraction phase.

G

grappling range—One of the three ranges of unarmed combat. Grappling range is the closest distance of unarmed combat from which you can employ a wide variety of close-quarter tools and techniques. The grappling range of unarmed combat is also divided into two planes: vertical (standing) and horizontal (ground fighting). See kicking range and punching range.

grappling-range tools—The various body tools and techniques that are employed in the grappling range of unarmed combat, including head butts; biting, tearing, clawing, crushing, and gouging tactics; foot stomps, horizontal, vertical, and diagonal elbow strikes, vertical and diagonal knee strikes, chokes, strangles, joint locks, and holds. See punching range tools and kicking range tools.

ground fighting—Also known as the horizontal grappling plane, this is fighting that takes place on the ground.

guard—Also known as the hand guard, this refers to a fighter's hand positioning.

guard position—Also known as leg guard or scissors hold, this is a ground-fighting position in which a fighter is on his back holding his opponent between his legs.

H

half beat – One of the four beat classifications in the Widow Maker Program. The half beat strike is delivered through the retraction phase of the proceeding strike.

hand positioning—See guard.

hand wraps—Long strips of cotton that are wrapped around the hands and wrists for greater protection.

haymaker—A wild and telegraphed swing of the arms executed by an unskilled fighter.

head-hunter—A fighter who primarily attacks the head.

heavy bag—A large cylindrical bag used to develop kicking, punching, or striking power.

high-line kick—One of the two different classifications of a kick. A kick that is directed to targets above an assailant's waist level. See low-line kick.

hip fusing—A full-contact drill that teaches a fighter to "stand his ground" and overcome the fear of exchanging blows with a stronger opponent. This exercise is performed by connecting two fighters with a 3-foot chain, forcing them to fight in the punching range of unarmed combat.

histrionics—The field of theatrics or acting.

hook kick—A circular kick that can be delivered in both kicking and punching ranges.

hook punch—A circular punch that can be delivered in both the punching and grappling ranges.

I

impact power—Destructive force generated by mass and velocity.

impact training—A training exercise that develops pain tolerance.

incapacitate—To disable an assailant by rendering him unconscious or damaging his bones, joints, or organs.

initiative—Making the first offensive move in combat.

inside position—The area between the opponent's arms, where he has the greatest amount of control.

intent—One of the essential factors to consider when assessing a threatening individual. The assailant's purpose or motive. See demeanor, positioning, range, and weapon capability.

intuition—The innate ability to know or sense something without the use of rational thought.

J

joint lock—A grappling-range technique that immobilizes the assailant's joint.

K

kick—A sudden, forceful strike with the foot.

kicking range—One of the three ranges of unarmed combat. Kicking range is the furthest distance of unarmed combat wherein you use your legs to strike an assailant. See grappling range and punching range.

kicking-range tools—The various body weapons employed in the kicking range of unarmed combat, including side kicks, push kicks, hook kicks, and vertical kicks.

killer instinct—A cold, primal mentality that surges to your consciousness and turns you into a vicious fighter.

kinesics—The study of nonlinguistic body movement communications. (For example, eye movement, shrugs, or facial gestures.)

kinesiology—The study of principles and mechanics of human movement.

kinesthetic perception—The ability to accurately feel your body during the execution of a particular movement.

knowledge—One of the three factors that determine who will win a street fight. Knowledge means knowing and understanding how to fight. See skills and attitude.

L

lead side -The side of the body that faces an assailant.

leg guard—See guard position.

linear movement—Movements that follow the path of a straight line.

low-maintenance tool—Offensive and defensive tools that require the least amount of training and practice to maintain proficiency. Low maintenance tools generally do not require preliminary stretching.

low-line kick—One of the two different classifications of a kick. A kick that is directed to targets below the assailant's waist level. (See high-line kick.)

lock—See joint lock.

M

maneuver—To manipulate into a strategically desired position.

MAP—An acronym that stands for moderate, aggressive, passive. MAP provides the practitioner with three possible responses to various grabs, chokes, and holds that occur from a standing position. See aggressive response, moderate response, and passive response.

martial arts—The "arts of war."

masking—The process of concealing your true feelings from your opponent by manipulating and managing your body language.

mechanics—(See body mechanics.)

mental attributes—The various cognitive qualities that enhance your fighting skills.

mental component—One of the three vital components of the CFA system. The mental component includes the cerebral aspects of fighting including the killer instinct, strategic and tactical development, analysis and integration, philosophy, and cognitive development. See physical component and spiritual component.

mesomorph—One of the three somatotypes. A body type classified by a high degree of muscularity and strength. The mesomorph possesses the ideal physique for unarmed combat. See ectomorph and endomorph.

mobility—A combative attribute. The ability to move your body quickly and freely while balanced. See footwork.

moderate response—One of the three possible counters when assaulted by a grab, choke, or hold from a standing position. Moderate response requires you to counter your opponent with a control and restraint (submission hold). See aggressive response and passive response.

modern martial art—A pragmatic combat art that has evolved to meet the demands and characteristics of the present time.

mounted position—A dominant ground-fighting position where a fighter straddles his opponent.

muscular endurance—The muscles' ability to perform the same motion or task repeatedly for a prolonged period of time.

muscular flexibility—The muscles' ability to move through maximum natural ranges.

muscular strength—The maximum force that can be exerted by a particular muscle or muscle group against resistance.

muscular/skeletal conditioning—An element of physical fitness that entails muscular strength, endurance, and flexibility.

N

naked choke—A throat choke executed from the chest to back position. This secure choke is executed with two hands and it can be performed while standing, kneeling, and ground fighting with the opponent.

neutralize—See incapacitate.

neutral zone—The distance outside the kicking range at which neither the practitioner nor the assailant can touch the other.

nonaggressive physiology—Strategic body language used prior to initiating a first strike.

nontelegraphic movement—Body mechanics or movements that do not inform an assailant of your intentions.

nuclear ground-fighting tools—Specific grappling range tools designed to inflict immediate and irreversible damage. Nuclear tools and tactics include biting tactics, tearing tactics, crushing tactics, continuous choking tactics, gouging techniques, raking tactics, and all striking techniques.

O

offense—The armed and unarmed means and methods of attacking a criminal assailant.

offensive flow—Continuous offensive movements (kicks, blows, and strikes) with unbroken continuity that ultimately neutralize or terminate the opponent. See compound attack.

offensive reaction time—The elapsed time between target selection and target impaction.

one-mindedness—A state of deep concentration wherein you are free from all distractions (internal and external).

ostrich defense—One of the biggest mistakes one can make when defending against an opponent. This is when the practitioner looks away from that which he fears (punches, kicks, and strikes). His mentality is, "If I can't see it, it can't hurt me."

P

pain tolerance—Your ability to physically and psychologically withstand pain.

panic—The second stage of fear; overpowering fear. See fright and terror.

parry—A defensive technique: a quick, forceful slap that redirects an assailant's linear attack. There are two types of parries: horizontal and vertical.

passive response—One of the three possible counters when assaulted by a grab, choke, or hold from a standing position. Passive response requires you to nullify the assault without injuring your adversary. See aggressive response and moderate response.

patience—A combative attribute. The ability to endure and tolerate difficulty.

perception—Interpretation of vital information acquired from your senses when faced with a potentially threatening situation.

philosophical resolution—The act of analyzing and answering various questions concerning the use of violence in defense of yourself and others.

philosophy—One of the five aspects of CFA's mental component. A deep state of introspection whereby you methodically resolve critical questions concerning the use of force in defense of yourself or others.

physical attributes—The numerous physical qualities that enhance your combative skills and abilities.

physical component—One of the three vital components of the CFA system. The physical component includes the physical aspects of fighting, such as physical fitness, weapon/technique mastery, and combative attributes. See mental component and spiritual component.

physical conditioning—See combative fitness.

physical fitness—See combative fitness.

positional asphyxia—The arrangement, placement, or positioning of your opponent's body in such a way as to interrupt your breathing and cause unconsciousness or possibly death.

positioning—The spatial relationship of the assailant to the assailed person in terms of target exposure, escape, angle of attack, and various other strategic considerations.

post-traumatic syndrome—A group of symptoms that may occur in the aftermath of a violent confrontation with a criminal assailant. Common symptoms of post-traumatic syndrome include denial, shock, fear, anger, severe depression, sleeping and eating disorders, societal withdrawal, and paranoia.

power—A physical attribute of armed and unarmed combat. The amount of force you can generate when striking an anatomical target.

power generators—Specific points on your body that generate impact power. There are three anatomical power generators: shoulders, hips, and feet.

precision—See accuracy.

preemptive strike—See first strike.

premise—An axiom, concept, rule, or any other valid reason to modify or go beyond that which has been established.

preparedness—A state of being ready for combat. There are three components of preparedness: affective preparedness, cognitive preparedness, and psychomotor preparedness.

probable reaction dynamics - The opponent's anticipated or predicted movements or actions during both armed and unarmed combat.

proficiency training—A CFA training methodology requiring the practitioner to execute a specific body weapon, technique, maneuver, or tactic over and over for a prescribed number of repetitions. See conditioning training and street training.

proxemics—The study of the nature and effect of man's personal space.

proximity—The ability to maintain a strategically safe distance from a threatening individual.

pseudospeciation—A combative attribute. The tendency to assign subhuman and inferior qualities to a threatening assailant.

psychological conditioning—The process of conditioning the mind for the horrors and rigors of real combat.

psychomotor preparedness—One of the three components of preparedness. Psychomotor preparedness means possessing all of the physical skills and attributes necessary to defeat a formidable adversary. See affective preparedness and cognitive preparedness.

punch—A quick, forceful strike of the fists.

punching range—One of the three ranges of unarmed combat. Punching range is the mid range of unarmed combat from which the fighter uses his hands to strike his assailant. See kicking range and grappling range.

punching-range tools—The various body weapons that are employed in the punching range of unarmed combat, including finger jabs, palm-heel strikes, rear cross, knife-hand strikes, horizontal and shovel hooks, uppercuts, and hammer-fist strikes. See grappling-range tools and kicking-range tools.

Q

qualities of combat—See attributes of combat.

quarter beat - One of the four beat classifications of the Widow Maker Program. Quarter beat strikes never break contact with the assailant's face. Quarter beat strikes are primarily responsible for creating the psychological panic and trauma when Razing.

R

range—The spatial relationship between a fighter and a threatening assailant.

range deficiency—The inability to effectively fight and defend in all ranges of combat (armed and unarmed).

range manipulation—A combative attribute. The strategic manipulation of combat ranges.

range proficiency—A combative attribute. The ability to effectively fight and defend in all ranges of combat (armed and unarmed).

ranges of engagement—See combat ranges.

ranges of unarmed combat—The three distances (kicking range, punching range, and grappling range) a fighter might physically engage with an assailant while involved in unarmed combat.

raze – To level, demolish or obliterate.

razer – One who performs the Razing methodology.

razing – The second phase of the Widow Maker Program. A series of vicious close quarter techniques designed to physically and psychologically extirpate a criminal attacker.

reaction dynamics—see probable reaction dynamics.

reaction time—The elapsed time between a stimulus and the response to that particular stimulus. See offensive reaction time and defensive reaction time.

rear cross—A straight punch delivered from the rear hand that crosses from right to left (if in a left stance) or left to right (if in a right stance).

rear side—The side of the body furthest from the assailant. See lead side.

reasonable force—That degree of force which is not excessive for a particular event and which is appropriate in protecting yourself or others.

refinement—The strategic and methodical process of improving or perfecting.

relocation principle—Also known as relocating, this is a street-fighting tactic that requires you to immediately move to a new location (usually by flanking your adversary) after delivering a compound attack.

repetition—Performing a single movement, exercise, strike, or action continuously for a specific period.

research—A scientific investigation or inquiry.

rhythm—Movements characterized by the natural ebb and flow of related elements.

ritual-oriented training—Formalized training that is conducted without intrinsic purpose. See combat-oriented training and sport-oriented training.

S

safety—One of the three criteria for a CFA body weapon, technique, maneuver, or tactic. It means that the tool, technique, maneuver or tactic provides the least amount of danger and risk for the practitioner. See efficiency and effectiveness.

scissors hold—See guard position.

self-awareness—One of the three categories of CFA awareness. Knowing and understanding yourself. This includes aspects of yourself which may provoke criminal violence and which will promote a proper and strong reaction to an attack. See criminal awareness and situational awareness.

self-confidence—Having trust and faith in yourself.

self-enlightenment—The state of knowing your capabilities, limitations, character traits, feelings, general attributes, and motivations. See self-awareness.

set—A term used to describe a grouping of repetitions.

shadow fighting—A CFA training exercise used to develop and refine your tools, techniques, and attributes of armed and unarmed combat.

situational awareness—One of the three categories of CFA awareness. A state of being totally alert to your immediate surroundings, including people, places, objects, and actions. (See criminal awareness and self-awareness.)

skeletal alignment—The proper alignment or arrangement of your body. Skeletal alignment maximizes the structural integrity of striking tools.

skills—One of the three factors that determine who will win a street fight. Skills refers to psychomotor proficiency with the tools and techniques of combat. See Attitude and Knowledge.

slipping—A defensive maneuver that permits you to avoid an assailant's linear blow without stepping out of range. Slipping can be accomplished by quickly snapping the head and upper torso sideways (right or left) to avoid the blow.

snap back—A defensive maneuver that permits you to avoid an assailant's linear and circular blows without stepping out of range. The snap back can be accomplished by quickly snapping the head backward to avoid the assailant's blow.

somatotypes—A method of classifying human body types or builds into three different categories: endomorph, mesomorph, and ectomorph. See endomorph, mesomorph, and ectomorph.

sparring—A training exercise where two or more fighters fight each other while wearing protective equipment.

speed—A physical attribute of armed and unarmed combat. The rate or a measure of the rapid rate of motion.

spiritual component—One of the three vital components of the CFA system. The spiritual component includes the metaphysical issues and aspects of existence. See physical component and mental component.

sport-oriented training—Training that is geared for competition and governed by a set of rules. See combat-oriented training and ritual-oriented training.

sprawling—A grappling technique used to counter a double- or single-leg takedown.

square off—To be face-to-face with a hostile or threatening assailant who is about to attack you.

stance—One of the many strategic postures you assume prior to or during armed or unarmed combat.

stick fighting—Fighting that takes place with either one or two sticks.

strategic positioning—Tactically positioning yourself to either escape, move behind a barrier, or use a makeshift weapon.

strategic/tactical development—One of the five elements of CFA's mental component.

strategy—A carefully planned method of achieving your goal of engaging an assailant under advantageous conditions.

street fight—A spontaneous and violent confrontation between two or more individuals wherein no rules apply.

street fighter—An unorthodox combatant who has no formal training. His combative skills and tactics are usually developed in the street by the process of trial and error.

street training—A CFA training methodology requiring the practitioner to deliver explosive compound attacks for 10 to 20 seconds. See condition ng training and proficiency training.

strength training—The process of developing muscular strength through systematic application of progressive resistance.

striking art—A combat art that relies predominantly on striking techniques to neutralize or terminate a criminal attacker.

striking shield—A rectangular shield constructed of foam and vinyl used to develop power in your kicks, punches, and strikes.

striking tool—A natural body weapon that impacts with the assailant's anatomical target.

strong side—The strongest and most coordinated side of your body.

structure—A definite and organized pattern.

style—The distinct manner in which a fighter executes or

performs his combat skills.

stylistic integration—The purposeful and scientific collection of tools and techniques from various disciplines, which are strategically integrated and dramatically altered to meet three essential criteria: efficiency, effectiveness, and combative safety.

submission holds—Also known as control and restraint techniques, many of these locks and holds create sufficient pain to cause the adversary to submit.

system—The unification of principles, philosophies, rules, strategies, methodologies, tools, and techniques of a particular method of combat.

T

tactic—The skill of using the available means to achieve an end.

target awareness—A combative attribute that encompasses five strategic principles: target orientation, target recognition, target selection, target impaction, and target exploitation.

target exploitation—A combative attribute. The strategic maximization of your assailant's reaction dynamics during a fight. Target exploitation can be applied in both armed and unarmed encounters.

target impaction—The successful striking of the appropriate anatomical target.

target orientation—A combative attribute. Having a workable knowledge of the assailant's anatomical targets.

target recognition—The ability to immediately recognize appropriate anatomical targets during an emergency self-defense situation.

target selection—The process of mentally selecting the

appropriate anatomical target for your self-defense situation. This is predicated on certain factors, including proper force response, assailant's positioning, and range.

target stare—A form of telegraphing in which you stare at the anatomical target you intend to strike.

target zones—The three areas in which an assailant's anatomical targets are located. (See zone one, zone two and zone three.)

technique—A systematic procedure by which a task is accomplished.

telegraphic cognizance—A combative attribute. The ability to recognize both verbal and non-verbal signs of aggression or assault.

telegraphing—Unintentionally making your intentions known to your adversary.

tempo—The speed or rate at which you speak.

terminate—To kill.

terror—The third stage of fear; defined as overpowering fear. See fright and panic.

timing—A physical and mental attribute of armed and unarmed combat. Your ability to execute a movement at the optimum moment.

tone—The overall quality or character of your voice.

tool—See body weapon.

traditional martial arts—Any martial art that fails to evolve and change to meet the demands and characteristics of its present environment.

traditional style/system—See traditional martial arts.

training drills—The various exercises and drills aimed at perfecting combat skills, attributes, and tactics.

U

unified mind—A mind free and clear of distractions and focused on the combative situation.

use of force response—A combative attribute. Selecting the appropriate level of force for a particular emergency self-defense situation.

V

viciousness—A combative attribute. The propensity to be extremely violent and destructive often characterized by intense savagery.

violence—The intentional utilization of physical force to coerce, injure, cripple, or kill.

visualization—Also known as mental visualization or mental imagery. The purposeful formation of mental images and scenarios in the mind's eye.

W

warm-up—A series of mild exercises, stretches, and movements designed to prepare you for more intense exercise.

weak side—The weaker and more uncoordinated side of your body.

weapon and technique mastery—A component of CFA's physical component. The kinesthetic and psychomotor development of a weapon or combative technique.

weapon capability—An assailant's ability to use and attack with a particular weapon.

webbing - The first phase of the Widow Maker Program.

The Widow Maker Program

Webbing is a two hand strike delivered to the assailant's chin. It is called Webbing because your hands resemble a large web that wraps around the enemy's face.

widow maker – One who makes widows by destroying husbands.

widow maker program – A CFA combat program specifically designed to teach the law abiding citizen how to use extreme force when faced with immediate threat of unlawful deadly criminal attack. The Widow Maker program is divided into two phases or methodologies: Webbing and Razing.

Y

yell—A loud and aggressive scream or shout used for various strategic reasons.

Z

zero beat – One of the four beat classifications of the Widow Maker Program. Zero beat strikes are full pressure techniques applied to a specific target until it completely ruptures. They include gouging, crushing, biting, and choking techniques.

zone one—Anatomical targets related to your senses, including the eyes, temple, nose, chin, and back of neck.

zone three—Anatomical targets related to your mobility, including thighs, knees, shins, and instep.

zone two—Anatomical targets related to your breathing, including front of neck, solar plexus, ribs, and groin.

About The Author

With over 30 years of experience, Sammy Franco is one of the world's foremost authorities on armed and unarmed self-defense. Highly regarded as a leading innovator in combat sciences, Mr. Franco was one of the premier pioneers in the field of "reality-based" self-defense and martial arts instruction.

Sammy Franco is perhaps best known as the founder and creator of Contemporary Fighting Arts (CFA), a state-of-the-art offensive-based combat system that is specifically designed for real-world self-defense. CFA is a sophisticated and practical system of self-defense, designed specifically to provide efficient and effective methods to avoid, defuse, confront, and neutralize both armed and unarmed attackers.

Sammy Franco has frequently been featured in martial art magazines, newspapers, and appeared on numerous radio and television programs. Mr. Franco has also authored numerous books, magazine articles and editorials, and has developed a popular library of instructional videos.

Sammy Franco's experience and credibility in the combat science is unequaled. One of his many accomplishments in this field includes the fact that he has earned the ranking of a Law Enforcement Master Instructor, and has designed, implemented, and taught officer survival training to the United States Border Patrol (USBP). He instructs members of the US Secret Service, Military Special Forces,

The Widow Maker Program

Washington DC Police Department, Montgomery County, Maryland Deputy Sheriffs, and the US Library of Congress Police. Sammy Franco is also a member of the prestigious International Law Enforcement Educators and Trainers Association (ILEETA) as well as the American Society of Law Enforcement Trainers (ASLET) and he is listed in the "Who's Who Director of Law Enforcement Instructors."

Sammy Franco is a nationally certified Law Enforcement Instructor in the following curricula: PR-24 Side-Handle Baton, Police Arrest and Control Procedures, Police Personal Weapons Tactics, Police Power Handcuffing Methods, Police Oleoresin Capsicum Aerosol Training (OCAT), Police Weapon Retention and Disarming Methods, Police Edged Weapon Countermeasures and "Use of Force" Assessment and Response Methods.

Mr. Franco holds a Bachelor of Arts degree in Criminal Justice from the University of Maryland. He is a regularly featured speaker at a number of professional conferences, and conducts dynamic and enlightening seminars on numerous aspects of self-defense and combat training.

For more information about Mr. Franco and his unique Contemporary Fighting Arts system, you can visit his website at: www.SammyFranco.com

If you liked this book, you will also want to read these:

MAXIMUM DAMAGE
Hidden Secrets Behind Brutal Fighting Combination
by Sammy Franco

Maximum Damage teaches you the quickest ways to beat your opponent in the street by exploiting his physical and psychological reactions in a fight. Learn how to stay two steps ahead of your adversary by knowing exactly how he will react to your strikes before they are delivered. In this unique book, reality based self-defense expert Sammy Franco reveals his unique Probable Reaction Dynamic (PRD) fighting method. Probable reaction dynamics are both a scientific and comprehensive offensive strategy based on the positional theory of combat. Regardless of your style of fighting, PRD training will help you overpower your opponent by seamlessly integrating your strikes into brutal fighting combinations that are fast, ferocious and final! 8.5 x 5.5, paperback, 240 photos, illustrations, 238 pages.

FIRST STRIKE
End a Fight in Ten Seconds or Less!
by Sammy Franco

Learn how to stop any attack before it starts by mastering the art of the preemptive strike. First Strike gives you an easy-to-learn yet highly effective self-defense game plan for handling violent close-quarter combat encounters. First Strike will teach you instinctive, practical and realistic self-defense techniques that will drop any criminal attacker to the floor with one punishing blow. By reading this book and by practicing, you will learn the hard-hitting skills necessary to execute a punishing first strike and ultimately prevail in a self-defense situation. And that's what it is all about: winning in as little time as possible. 8.5 x 5.5, paperback, photos, illustrations, 202 pages.

OUT OF THE CAGE
A Complete Guide to Beating a Mixed Martial Artist on the Street
by Sammy Franco

Forget the UFC! The truth is, a street fight is the "ultimate no holds barred fight" often with deadly consequences, but you don't need to join a mixed martial arts school or become a cage fighter to defeat a mixed martial artist on the street. What you need are solid skills and combat proven techniques that can be applied under the stress of real world combat conditions. Out of the Cage takes you inside the mind of the MMA fighter and reveals all of his weaknesses, allowing you to quickly exploit them to your advantage. 10 x 7, paperback, photos, illustrations, 194 pages.

WAR MACHINE
How to Transform Yourself Into A Vicious & Deadly Street Fighter
by Sammy Franco

War Machine is a book that will change you for the rest of your life! When followed accordingly, War Machine will forge your mind, body and spirit into iron. Once armed with the mental and physical attributes of the War Machine, you will become a strong and confident warrior that can handle just about anything that life may throw your way. In essence, War Machine is a way of life. Powerful, intense, and hard. 11 x 8.5, paperback, photos, illustrations, 210 pages.

THE COMPLETE BODY OPPONENT BAG BOOK
by Sammy Franco

In this one-of-a-kind book, world-renowned martial arts expert, Sammy Franco teaches you the many hidden training features of the body opponent bag that will improve your fighting skills and accelerate your fitness and conditioning. Develop explosive speed and power, improve your endurance, and tone, and strengthen your entire body. With detailed photographs, step-by-step instructions, and dozens of unique workout routines, The Complete Body Opponent Bag Book is the authoritative resource for mastering this lifelike punching bag. 8.5 x 5.5, paperback, photos, illustrations, 206 pages.

WHEN SECONDS COUNT
Self-Defense for the Real World
by Sammy Franco

When Seconds Count is a comprehensive street smart self-defense book instructing law abiding citizens how to protect themselves against the mounting threat of violent crime. When Seconds Count is considered by many to be one of the best books on real world self-defense instruction. Ideal for men and women of all ages who are serious about taking responsibility for their own safety. By studying the concepts and techniques taught in this book, you will feel a renewed sense of empowerment, enabling you to live your life with greater confidence and personal freedom. 10 x 7, paperback, photos, illustrations, 208 pages.

CONTEMPORARY FIGHTING ARTS, LLC
"Real World Self-Defense Since 1989"
www.SammyFranco.com
301-279-2244

Finis

51025780R00122

Made in the USA
Lexington, KY
09 April 2016